Days Like This

Days Like This

A Portrait of Scotland Through the Stories of its People

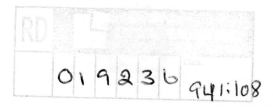

Luath Press Limited

EDINBURGH

www.luath.co.uk

First published 2009

in association with Scottish Book Trust

ISBN 978-1-906307-97-4

The paper used in this book is neutral sized and recyclable.
It is made from elemental chlorine free pulps sourced
from renewable forests.

Printed and bound by
CPI Bookmarque, Croydon CRO 4TD

Typeset in 10.5 point Sabon
by 3btype.com

Photo credits:
Cover: Ignasi Buch (main), Marion Bourbouze, Stewart Bremner
Back: David Gillanders, Pascal Saez, James Wilson

Contents

Society

Tough Times

Sports and Travel

Acknowledgements

Days Like This is the culmination of a project run by Scottish Book Trust. Scottish Book Trust is the leading agency for the promotion of literature in Scotland, developing innovative projects to encourage adults and children to read, write and be inspired by books. It is a not-for-profit organisation, funded by Scottish Arts Council, sponsorship and other grants, and is based at the heart of Edinburgh's literature quarter on the Royal Mile. For more information, go to: www.scottishbooktrust.com

Scottish Book Trust would like to thank the following people and organisations: its partners at the BBC – Lindsay Gillies, Helen Wolfenden, Jane Fowler and David Stenhouse; its celebrity curators – Jamie Andrew, Evelyn Glennie, Hardeep Singh Kohli, Siobhan Redmond, Irvine Welsh and Roddy Woomble; The Scottish Arts Council Lottery Fund for supporting the project; and its team of readers Marion Bourbouze, Jo Burnside, Paul Gallagher, Olivier Joly, Michael Merillo and Clare Rodgers.

Introduction

WE LIVE IN A story-saturated age, but one in which the professional is dominant.

Scottish Book Trust set out to prove the opposite, that it could be the voices of ordinary people which drew the crowds and lingered on the air. With the help of BBC Radio Scotland and six 'celebrity curators', we solicited true stories from ordinary voices, sure of finding them extraordinary. Why? Because when a story has a direct connection with a life, the sincerity and spontaneity of the telling tends to make an indelible impression on the reader.

The aim of *Days Like This* was to try to capture the ordinary genius we knew was out there in Scotland, tapping into the inexhaustible reservoir of experience that makes up a nation. Echoing Liz Lochhead's famous question: 'Country: Scotland. Whit like is it?' the answers have come back to us, vivid and enthralling. A bald 16 stone cross-dressing rugby player; a boy whose favourite pet is a brick; a haunted pub basement; a frightening ride with Fred West; a love affair that begins outside a burning disco – these are just some of the stories included here, every one a gem.

But that's by no means all.

I have several favourites that never made it into this short selection, and you might feel the same if you go to our website at www.scottishbooktrust.com/dayslikethis where all of the submissions – over 800 in total – are available. Uniformly well told, these stories form a higgledy-piggledy map of Scotland, and so of the common humanity which binds us to ourselves, and to the rest of the world.

They say that life is stranger than fiction, and it's true – read on and find out for yourself.

Marc Lambert
Chief Executive of Scottish Book Trust

Curators' Stories

NORTH SEA YACHT RACE

Jamie Andrew

AS *MRS CHIPPY* LEAVES the great glacier carved bay of Stavanger and moves out into the North Sea, it's startling how quickly the conditions change. The pleasant breeze which played round our sheltered fjord now becomes a powerful wind and the surface of the sea rises up in a relentless procession of choppy waves, big and unpredictable.

I haven't even had a chance to change into my sailing gear so I duck down below to pull it on. Almost immediately the nausea hits me as the boat, pitching and rolling wildly, throws me around the cramped cabin while I wrestle with the waterproofs.

I make it back on deck feeling very green, but in fact it's our skipper, Stuart, who is first to succumb. He is sitting at the chart table, attempting to plot our course, but has to break off to retch into a bucket. He emerges on deck looking grim, his face the pallor of a corpse.

Before long Alan also reaches for the bucket. As dusk approaches, we begin our watches, each taking two hours at the helm, followed by two hours on standby, huddled under the spray hood, and then two hours down below, trying to sleep. The two hours down below are the worst – the motion of the boat is absolutely unbearable, and the sea-sickness becomes all encompassing. It engenders in me a strange desperation. It's more than wishing that I was not on the boat, more even than wishing myself dead – I simply wish that I didn't exist at all. I am uncertain that I can bear another moment of this. Looking at their faces, I guess that Alan and Stuart feel the same way.

At 2.00 a.m. I rise from my tortured slumber, brave the heads for a pee, retch into the bucket, struggle back into my cold, wet waterproofs, and stagger up on deck. Stuart passes me wordlessly as he descends to his bed while Alan makes way for me at the helm and without further ado curls up foetus-like in the cockpit.

Suddenly, in the pitch black of night, I feel very out of my depth. Despite missing a hand and a foot respectively, Stuart and Alan are great sailors and I rely heavily on their experience. But now I am in charge of the boat and the conditions are quite frightening. The forecast force five and six winds have materialised as force six and seven, gusting eight, and the sea is very rough. The wind is blowing from the south-east – ideal for our westerly course, but it does mean that the waves are approaching from behind us. As each wave arrives, invisible in the dark, it lifts our little boat right up to its crest, at which point we either slump back down the other side, or, if we time it just right, we surf down the front of the wave, gathering speed and shooting off down the trough.

The trouble is that without being able to see the waves, it is very difficult to do this and I have to rely on the feel of the boat and the feel of the wheel as I heave it from side to side. It's a real physical job and balancing is difficult, bracing my prosthetic legs across the cockpit and clinging to the wheel with my already bruised stumps.

The huge waves often catch me by surprise and break over the back of the boat, drenching us and sending the boat crashing down into the gutter below. Then, without warning, a monster. I can sense the boat rising way up high, then before I know it we are falling, rushing down the steep face of the wave at a startling velocity.

The boat smashes into the bottom of the wave and tips over alarmingly. The starboard side plunges into the rushing water and it seems certain that we must be knocked down flat.

Alan, curled up on the port side of the boat, is hurled bodily across the cockpit and before his safety line can come tight he smashes into the portside winch and the guard rails.

In that moment, time seems to stand still. I see Alan, pinned by gravity against the rails, which are ploughing through the water as the boat heaves over into the sea, but I'm not thinking about him, or myself, or Stuart. I'm thinking about Jim. Jim, who was such an experienced sailor, so competent, so self-assured, yet who had been caught off-guard by just such a wave, somewhere in the sea north of Iceland, less than two years ago. Knocked overboard, swallowed up by the inky black sea, Jim was never seen again. Such a good friend. Such a tragic loss.

And now I'm thinking about myself. Already brutally scarred by tragedy, I survived, went on to rebuild, to marry, to have children. And now here I am again on the brink of disaster. I don't want it to be this way. I don't want to die like this. I don't want the sea to have me.

And then the moment is past. *Mrs Chippy* doesn't topple over but rights herself. Alan falls back into the cockpit, clutching at his badly bruised arm. Stuart rushes up from below to see what on earth has happened. We sail on into the night.

By dawn the wind has dropped slightly and the sea eased. We are making great progress and as the boat skims across the surface of the water, it is already becoming hard to imagine the fear and turmoil of the previous night. Life is good again, the sailing a sheer joy and the spirit of adventure courses through my veins.

The sea-sickness has lessened and we manage a revitalizing brew. A school of dolphins joins us, leaping playfully alongside and across our bow wave. We sail on towards the horizon, to Scotland and home.

Go to page 143 to read Jamie's favourite story.

DAME TODAY, GONE TOMORROW

Evelyn Glennie

MY DAY BEGAN in another time zone, with a dash away from New York where I had just given a speech to a conference of 1,500 women. My timescale was very tight. As I crossed the Atlantic I experienced terror, panic and concern. Would the plane land on time? Would the dress I had chosen for this special day arrive? And would I get there in time?

As we landed at Heathrow it suddenly occurred to me that the dress might not fit properly, and I did not have a plan B. As I passed through customs I found my driver and there he was with the dress. I rushed to change into it. It had been created specially for the occasion in a wonderful red which fitted – to my relief – beautifully.

It's amazing how nervousness makes the senses razor sharp. I began to absorb everything that was happening around me. The driver was weaving his way through the dense London traffic to Buckingham Palace. My nervousness grew. Pearls of perspiration rolled down my back. As we approached the gates I looked out for my mum and the team from the office. But I couldn't see them anywhere! Total panic – then I spotted them.

The grandeur of the occasion suddenly hit me. I took a look around, marvelling at the palace décor, and thought of the incredible history of these rooms. My mum gave me a hug – I thought she was going to cry! And my team – how different they looked, all smart and spruce and visibly relieved I had arrived on time. I wanted so much for them to be with me – I simply could not achieve as much without them. Getting this award had been mostly about teamwork.

Then I was jolted back to reality. It's my time. I walk carefully to my place and kneel before the Queen, hyper-aware. Is that a thread I can feel catching on my dress? My shoes are new – I hope they don't squeak. I try to concentrate, to take in the atmosphere and the faces around me. I don't want to miss a second of this magical day.

As I stand in front of the Queen my heart is beating so loudly I am sure it can be heard by Her Majesty. I can barely hear myself think! Luckily, I can lip read and am currently learning to sign. But none of these extra skills seem to help as I stand before one of the world's most powerful women. I am really anxious as I accept my award.

I have met the Queen before, but on this occasion I feel a sense of awe as I walk towards her. She looks so grand and yet so approachable. For me she is hugely inspiring in her graciousness and her continued interest in my work. We exchange a few words. She gives me a wonderful sense of caring, which I will treasure for the rest of my life.

Such a feeling! As I take my place amongst the other people who have come for their award I sense I am somehow floating amidst a sea of faces. Some I recognise, others I do not. I feel exhilarated and yet humbled. My award is for Services to Music. It has been hard work for me to overcome my deafness and convince others I can do it, but now here I am in this esteemed setting. For me there can be no greater experience of reward than this.

As a child I only knew that I wanted to be me, not famous or a celebrity, just me. I loved playing music then, as much as now, and the excitement and curiosity of performing solo or with others is still the same. What I realize more profoundly now is that music and the arts truly can make a difference in people's lives.

I have never mourned the loss of my hearing but instead embraced the opportunity to learn how to listen in a different way. The vibrations of my instruments have been with me for many years and I am still on a journey of discovery.

Suddenly, we are being ushered out of the magnificent room and I am being reminded that I need to make a move. I rush off back to the airport. No time to stop and dwell on the occasion just yet, I have to get to my next performance in Italy!

To receive any award is wonderful but to attend an Investiture is a unique honour. As I stand there watching others receive their awards, especially those members of the military recognised for their bravery on behalf of their country, I feel very humble. After all, I am lucky by comparison; my life has been enriched by so many others including my family, the public, composers, and members and musicians of so many orchestras, all of whom have shared their time and efforts with me.

As I climb the steps to the plane, I stop and pinch myself. Did this really happen? I look round and my heart is filled with pride. This is my country and I am proud to accept this award. Even though the day was so hectic and far too short, it was also the most memorable of my whole life.

As a little girl growing up on a farm near Aberdeen I could not have dreamed that this day would come. Never in my life could I have guessed that one day I would become Dame Evelyn Glennie.

Go to page 194 to read Evelyn's favourite story.

THE SHINIEST HIPPOPOTAMUS
THAT I HAVE EVER SEEN

Siobhan Redmond

THERE'S ONLY ONE THING I do regularly that I'm sure my parents would approve of: I look up new words in the dictionary. Throughout my childhood, as soon as I'd say, 'What does this word mean?' I'd be told to find out for myself. Words are important to my family – as things of beauty, weapons of choice and tools for telling a story. My parents grew up in households where everyone told stories to and about everyone else and I grew up surrounded by that tradition.

In fact I'm still surrounded by it: my bedroom is in the roof, and in the eaves on either side of my bed are boxes packed with diaries, stories, poems and letters written by my parents, my granny and my aunts. Some boxes have lain unopened for many years. As people died, as people will do, my sister Grainne and I pack up what seems personal and promise ourselves to look at it later. It's sore reading and yet impossible to dispose of. It's become buried treasure – part of me like bones.

My wonderful, hilarious rose-scented Aunt Mary is responsible for much of the archive. She deserves another audience, and so today, I finally look in the eaves for a story of hers to send in her name to Days Like This, a project she would have approved of.

She had exciting stories from the steelworks where she was a nurse, tales of gore and fire and furnaces and of how men were when they forgot she was a woman. She could turn anything into a better version of itself. I see her as she is in her stories: eating roasted cheese cooked on a shovel thrust for an instant into an industrial oven; laughing with her pal Annie Park as they snipped the feather off an obtrusive hat worn by a woman sat in front of them at the theatre; fainting at her own reflection in a darkened window, or at any mouse; dressed up as a ghost and lying in wait for my sister, my cousins and me to scare us into that delicious state where you shriek and laugh till your breath sticks and even your hair hurts.

Her boxes are at the front, and so I lug those out into the bedroom, in for a penny, in for a pound, hell slap it into me, why not go further back? Here's a letter from Granny about her home help and a steakpie…Granny had stories about the Black and Tans, of run-ins with her scary mother-in-law Katie Roberts who was one of the Drinking Redmonds and owner of a dog-killing cat called Tiddles, of giving birth to my dad on a table. 'An awfy girny wean,' she said. 'Aye greetin'.'

He grew up to be a spectacular dandy with velveteen suits, long hair, a beautiful face, a wicked way with words and a story for everyone. This last incensed my mother who preferred to keep a low profile – all the better to surprise people. She was in fact the star storyteller; by far the best actor in the family with a leaning towards the tragic, she'd stun us through tears into silence if she felt like it. She took no prisoners and gave me whatever theatrical ability I have.

We had to have stories, my sister and me. I wouldn't eat till I'd heard about, for instance, the fish that swam from Norway with a fishcake for my dinner balanced on its head. Grainne was worse – she'd only eat if her food was turned, spoonful by spoonful, into mystery parcels.

'Who's this for, Grainne?'

'For me.'

'What's in it?'

'A Grandfather to make Daddy eat things he doesn't like.'

In search of more stories I go right back into the narrow space behind the shoeboxes, spare duvets and Christmas decorations. I cut the packing tape on the furthest box and, under the school reports ('Could do better if tried harder.'), the ancient photos of Grainne with pigtails and me with a knicker-pink eye patch, I find my reward.

Much as I hate it when the tupenny-ha'penny advice from every agony aunt turns out to be right, it seems true enough that if you grit your teeth and do the thing you dread, you get a prize. And mine is going through these boxes and finding a thing I thought I'd lost forever except in barely remembered fragments, a song my dad wrote when I was really wee. I'd had a story book about a baby hippo: its final line describing him after his evening bath inspired dad to create a sparklier lyric which was sung to the tune of John Brown's Body.

Here, written out in my dad's spidery hand is 'The Shiniest

Hippopotamus that I Have Ever Seen'. I'm so happy to have this back – thrilled to see that the forgotten lines contain a word for me to look up – grateful to my family for their stories making this story. I remember us singing this as we drank baby coffee with lots of milk from little glass cups with wooden handles. You won't hear my dad harmonising in his pentatonic whisky tenor, but I do.

> The shiniest hippopotamus that I have ever seen
> Wore a purple tartan waistcoat and his eyes were emerald green
> His mouth glowed like a furnace; his comedos shone like stars
> And his teeth were ivory bars.
>
> Hip hip hip hippo hippo hippopotamus, (sung three times)
> And his teeth were ivory bars.
>
> His jaw lit like a lantern and his nose shone like a torch
> And if you went too near him then your eyebrows he would
>   scorch,
> His breath was like a blowlamp, his eyes blazed fierce and
>   bright
> And his tail lit up at night.
>
> Hip hip hip hippo hippo hippopotamus, (sung three times)
> And his tail lit up at night.

Go to page 121 to read Siobhan's favourite story.

GREY KNEE SOCKS

Hardeep Singh Kohli

A PAIR OF SOCKS. Grey knee socks. With a red and blue stripe around the top. That's how Pickle and I met. 1974. August. Hillhead. The West End of Glasgow. The first day of the local primary school and Pickle's mum and my mum found themselves at the back of the school hall, two immigrant wives with five-year-old sons and no knee socks (the ones with the red and blue stripes around the top). The only ones without knee socks. That wasn't the sole defining factor of the two families: we were the only brown faces in the room. Pickle Pathak and me, A. J. Ghujral, and our mothers. Like Morecambe and Wise's mothers; or Caesar and Brutus's mothers; maybe even Lennon and McCartney's mothers. Were there ever stronger grounds for bonding? A pair of grey knee socks. That was one thing about the immigrants; poor they may have been, but their kids were always going to look the part. You could always tell the immigrant kids: they had every item on the school uniform list, no matter how insignificant, they had to have it. It was a pride thing.

Registration over on the fateful day in Hillhead in the nearly mid-70s, our mothers left the school hall with fresh plans to acquire knee socks. But not before one of them won the battle to invite the other round for a sweet hot cup of masala tea. That too was another astonishing aspect of immigrant life. It was 'lift crisis culture'. In the ordinary run of play, in India, the Pathaks and the Ghujrals would never be friends. Their lives would run on two non-intersecting paths. There would be no familial concurrence, no shared existence, no pooled resource. The Ghujrals would be the middle-class aspirant affluent aristos of Delhi society; the Pathaks would probably run a small radio repair shop in a small street in a small town inhabited by small people. In the inevitable wave of the TV and VCR revolution they would probably be destroyed; then Manji, Mrs Pathak, would be forced into domestic service, as would the boys. Pathak Sahib would cultivate and develop a fantastically self-destructive drink problem and come home every evening drunk and bitter and full of regret, and visit his personal despair through his fists on his wife. But here in the great melting pot of British immigrant culture, finding themselves stuck between floors in the lift of life with each other, the Pathaks and the Ghujrals were forced to meet and bond. And they met and bonded.

Playing in the one room that the Pathak family lived in, I was painfully aware that Pickle and I had no great desire to be friends. I felt Pickle smelled. It was a feeling rather than a conclusively substantiated fact. Nonetheless, I felt he smelled. This was both harsh and fair. Pickle carried about with him the aroma of curried fish. It was both pungent and subtle. At first I found it difficult to establish where exactly the smell originated from. The entire room and all its belongings seem to share the same sharp aroma. And what an aroma; it was unmistakably marked by a rare and exotic quality. It was a smell that did not readily exist on the radar of West End of Glasgow smells; yet the nuance, the layers of the smell offered a certain complexity, a challenge that did not at first suggest fish. There was essence of bay, a suggestion of turmeric, the merest hint of cardamom. That smell was a conundrum wrapped in a mystery shrouded in enigma. Notwithstanding this esotericism, Pickle was smelly. And smelliness is next to Oh My Godliness. To be friends with such a child suggested more than just social liability.

Therefore, not being part of the cure, I realised on that very first day that I would have to become part of the problem. I would have to join the inevitable massed rank of smell detectors and with a cruelty children share with malign dictators, I would conduct the slagging of my 'friend' on a thrice daily basis: morning break, lunchtime and afternoon break.

Go to page 155 to read Hardeep's favourite story.

MY SPECIAL DAY

Irvine Welsh

IT WAS A FROZEN DAY in March at Hampden Park, where I was heading to see Hibs play in the League Cup final. But I was coming from Miami, with a pair of sunglasses and a light T-shirt and jeans, and a plastic bag containing a thick fleece and jacket. I flew in on Saturday night and was glad of the plastic bag and its contents when I disembarked on Sunday morning in Glasgow. I took a taxi into town. My UK mobile wasn't charged, so I had no way of contacting the boys on the bus coming through from Edinburgh.

It was a typical cold and driech winter Glasgow Sunday morning, and everything was shut. I had time to kill and decided that the best way to get re-orientated was to walk towards Hampden. I crossed the Clyde and headed south, stopping at a McDonald's for the first time in years, drinking a coffee. It had started to snow heavily. I had just come from 90 degree heat and I was feeling the absence of every one of them. That sicky jetlagged feeling hit me hard; like being on drugs but without the buzz.

At 12.30 p.m. a pub close to the ground had opened its doors. I was in there for a just a few minutes when my pals Tam and Russell came in with their dad, uncle and some friends. The pub started to quickly fill up with Hibernian and Kilmarnock supporters. I got talking to some lads from Ayrshire – they were good guys and we had a drink and a sing-song together and wished each other all the best. My jetlag was starting to recede. Tam had his phone and I was able to rendevous with the rest of the boys outside the ground and pick up my precious match ticket.

The jetlag kicked in again with a vengeance when I got inside the stadium, where 30,000 Hibs fans and 20,000 Killie supporters were creating an electric atmosphere. I felt a bit disconnected from everything and I suppose the drinks in the pub didn't help. But the fatigue left me in the second half as the goals started to fly in. As that half progressed it was evident that it was going to be Hibs' day, but Kilmarnock fans continued to back their team. Personally, I never felt totally safe, even at 3–1, you just don't when you follow Hibs, and I didn't relax till the other two goals hit the net. But we were treated to some great striking from Benji and Fletch, and 5–1 in a cup final is always a great result. While we deserved to win, the score line was a bit harsh on Killie, as it can be in cup finals when you just have to go for it if you're behind.

We watched the cup being presented, and people were singing but had that slightly out-of-it air of unreality, like it hadn't quite sunk in yet. Me perhaps more than most, with my head still in Miami. But I'd felt the same way back in 1991 when we beat Dunfermline and I was too young to remember that much detail about the 1972 win over Celtic, though I was there with my dad.

We sang our lungs out, 'Sunshine On Leith', then got on the bus back to the port. It was a brilliant atmosphere heading along the M8. Our great buddy Tich Grant had died suddenly and unexpectedly just a few weeks earlier and we had a banner in tribute to him. It was a great night back in Leith, but strange not to have the Wee Man there, and it was bittersweet thinking about him. This game started the cult of Tich's banner though – it's now been all over the world. I left the party at 5.00 a.m. and walked up Princes Street. I was planning to get an early morning train through to Glasgow but Waverley Station was locked up as it was still too early. I met a couple of boys who were finishing their shift as electricians and they very kindly gave me a lift back to Glasgow. I got the connecting flight to London then the transatlantic to Miami.

My friend Kenny was working over in Miami at the dance music festival and couldn't get back for the game. With the time differences I was able to present him with the Scottish newspapers on Monday morning at Jerry's Famous Deli in Miami Beach. I didn't have any jet lag at all by this time, but I indulged in a large Bloody Mary to toast the League Cup win. It was a great Hibs team, brought on by Tony Mowbray, with the win executed by John Collins. We knew they would be breaking up soon, due to financial problems, but it was great that they won something for us before doing so.

An exhausting day, but one I'll always remember. Let's have another, please, Mixu.

Go to page 65 to read Irvine's favourite story.

BRICK

Roddy Woomble

IN THE SUMMER of 1982 I lived in a town called Cournon d'Auvergne in the middle of France. My parents owned a Volkswagen camper van and we'd idle away the weekends and holidays driving around the French and Swiss countryside, stopping and setting up camp wherever we felt like it. I was six years old. It was the perfect way to spend summertime.

The van was compact and slept the whole family. There was a tent that attached onto its side, giving us extra room and somewhere to sit if it started to rain. The tent was heavy and clumsy to put up and always worked my father up into an aggravated fluster. Often the ground was hard and getting the tent pegs into it was even harder. Somewhere along the way he had picked up an old red brick to help him hammer in the pegs. The brick travelled with us in the bottom of the tent bag, and became an integral part in setting up camp. I took an instant liking for battering tent pegs into the ground with the brick. I was in charge of the brick's other job too, which consisted of him being tied loosely to the bottles of milk and lemonade so that they wouldn't float away when we left them cooling in the river.

It wasn't long before Brick and I were pretty tight. I found a long piece of string, which I threaded through one of his three holes and tied leaving a length so that I could pull him along behind me. We'd go for walks together around any campsite we were staying in. Me and Brick. Sometimes other adult campers would look up from their newspapers and smile at the simple picture; a six-year-old boy taking a brick for a walk around a campsite on a lead. Other children I met on site seemed initially curious of Brick, thinking that I might have something wrong with me, wondering why I had a brick for a pet. But they soon took a fondness for him. Some even found their own pet bricks.

One day, toward the end of the holiday, in Austria, in a campsite high in the Alps, Dad was hammering away, trying to get the final peg in a particularly hard piece of ground. All of a sudden Brick broke into four pieces. It wasn't my father's fault. The ground was hard as concrete and the pegs were bending. Brick had his work cut out. He'd taken one hit too many. Dad laid him on the ground. The lead was still attached to one of the broken pieces. We buried him in that evening, the service was brief and afterwards mum heated up a tin of ravioli on the camp stove and we ate it admiring how neatly the tent pegs had gone into the ground. Brick had done one good last job that was for sure. That was the last time I ever had a pet, that day up in the Austrian Alps. I've never wanted one since.

Go to page 159 to read Roddy's favourite story.

Childhood

CHRISTMAS 1957

Danny Adair

ME AND MA were in the living room making paper chains from old papers and magazines, trying to brighten the place up a bit. We lived in a tenement single end, one of the ones that hadn't fallen down yet, where three families shared one toilet on the landing.

I had never had a proper Christmas present. The best to date had been a homemade wooden sword, but this year there had been wee hints that there might be something a bit special. I really wanted a toy train. I had seen one, a Triang, in a toy shop, and dreamed about it every night.

Da wasn't home from work yet and although Ma was sunny and bright, and was teasing me, I caught her a couple of times glancing at the clock.

I was packed off to sleep in the bed recess, while she listened to a programme on the radio.

It took me a while to get to sleep, as I was excited and was trying to work out if it was really Santa himself that would bring my present, or if he just passed it to Ma. After I while I woke up to the sound of raised voices. It took me a bit to get my bearings and then I realised it was Christmas. Excitedly, I stuck my head through the curtains of the bed recess and I saw two things. A beautiful toy train laid out on the floor, with a ring, a tinplate track and a clockwork engine and two trucks. The way it was positioned, I could see every detail as I peered out. The other thing I saw was Da swinging Ma about by her hair and battering her with his fist.

He was yelling something about her stealing from his pockets, and about all the sacrifices he had made. I dived back into the recess before he saw me and covered my head with the pillow. I do remember hearing a roar and what sounded like something being dropped.

When I woke up on Christmas day proper, I peeped through the recess, and saw him sprawled on a chair, snoring like the old pig he was, and Ma, curled up in the other chair sobbing gently. I could see the bruising on her face would be really bad this time, and her eye was already almost closed.

In the far corner lay the remnants of my beautiful toy train, which had been crushed by his tackity boots and then disintegrated when he booted it into the corner.

I learned later that when he finished work, he had gone to the pub with his cronies, to 'celebrate Christmas'. They had stayed until closing time, and then gone for fish and chips, most of which ended up on his clothes rather than in his belly. Then his 'celebrations' had taken him to a carol service. It seems he always went to a Protestant one, but only because it was easier to rob the collection there. While being ejected for this larceny, he managed to knock some things over and throw up in the church entrance.

Years later in secondary school, one of the Brothers set us an essay. It was meant to motivate and be inspirational. The topic was 'When I grow up I want to...' and my essay had only 11 words.

'When I grow up I want to kill my old man'. Being good Christians they beat the crap out of me.

Christmas? Nah, I don't think so.

GOING HOME

Melvin Barnes

LOADS OF KIDS STAY in Canaan Lodge. You should see the rush to get in to breakfast in the morning. Not on Saturdays of course. Saturday there's no school. And that's the funny thing about school. I mean we all get on to the bus in the morning to go to school, which is not too bad. The bus I mean. Not school. I hate school. I hate Canaan Lodge. So anyway the bus takes us to school. When you come back at night you're not allowed to get off the bus, well not straight away. One of the grown-ups comes on with a load of books under their arms. If you get handed a book then you stay on the bus. Then you get taken to Red Hall. Well at least that's what the other kids say. They never tell you in the morning that you will be staying on the bus.

Breakfast was OK. I like breakfast especially on a Saturday. Saturday is the day we all get sixpence. When it came to my turn I took my sixpence from Nurse Cosgrove. They're all called nurses in Canaan Lodge. I expect it's because they all look like nurses. Anyway I stuck my sixpence into my dungarees and ran outside. I jumped on Topper and went lickety-split for the front gate and out into Canaan Lane. I was going home to my mum.

Have you ever noticed when you're not hungry and the sun is really warm that it gives you a really braw feeling? I took a good look for bandits before taking Topper up Morningside Road. The road was busy with grown-ups and tram cars. I like tram cars, they're a really braw colour. They're maroon. That's 'The Hearts' colours. The 'Jam Tarts' Uncle Bill calls them. I like the shoogly sparky way they go along the road.

Trams are good for finding your way to Uncle Bill's. You just follow the tram and look for the clock at Tollcross and then the clock at Haymarket. Tollcross is really busy. Before you get to Haymarket you have to gallop along Prince's Street. The fruit shop in Prince's Street was selling plums. I reached into my pocket but there was only a hole where my tanner should have been.

I was really hungry and if I grabbed a plum I could be halfway to Haymarket 'afore you could say 'Hopalong Cassidy'. Until I remembered what Mum and Uncle Bill said: 'Stealing wisnae right.' Crivvens! Then I saw the policeman out of the corner of my eye, but I'm good at running. A quick skelp across the road, a loup onto Topper's back and I was well on my way to Haymarket. I looked back but no-one was following.

I stopped at the Caley Picture house to see what picture was showing. It was one about cattle rustling and Glen Ford was in it. I love cowboy pictures. Hopalong Cassidy pictures I like the best. I wondered if Uncle Bill might take me to see it when I told him I could have stolen a plum but didn't.

The person who built those houses must be really clever. I'll tell you why. My uncle Bill lives at number 14 on the second storey up. You can ring the bell to his house from downstairs so that by the time you get up there my uncle has come to the door and is standing there saying, 'So it's you then, Melvin'. I think that is really clever, do you no. Well I rang the bell and just wheeched up them stairs only this time when I got to the door it wasn't Uncle Bill standing there. It was the Matron from Canaan Lodge.

My mum and Aunt Emma were sitting beside the Matron. They were all eating cakes from a wee plate and drinking tea. Grown-ups are always drinking tea and eating cakes so that was no surprise. What was a surprise was Mum saying to Matron, 'Aye he'll have to go back with you to Canaan Lodge.' I couldn't believe my ears.

Uncle Bill sat beside me and looked right at me. 'It's not so bad, young man,' he said. 'Your Mum needs to work. It'll no be for forever.'

He stood up and said, 'Here turn round and we'll put this coat on you for the journey home.' Well I did. When a grown-up tells you to do something then you just do it. That's the way it is.

So with Mum and Uncle Bill standing in the doorway shouting down the stairs 'I'll come and see you tomorrow with some comics' and me walking down the stair with Matron I didn't know what to do. I could have run away I suppose but I was far overtired for that. Not to mention still hungry. I wondered if I would get any tea when I got back to Canaan Lodge. I hate being a bairn. I can't wait to be older.

I got a big row for running away and causing a lot of worry. And I didn't get any tea. When I got into the dormitory all the other kids were asleep. Before climbing into bed I noticed that all of the lockers had a Sunday suit hanging from their rail. Then I remembered that it was Sunday school tomorrow.

I just lay there looking at my Sunday suit, my tummy rumbling and rumbling. Then I thought about what God would think when I went to Sunday school in the morning. I wondered if he would have minded if I had stolen one of those plums. Maybe he would smite me down like my Sunday school teacher said. Then I thought no. I've seen pictures of God in the Kirk and he looks really kind. I rolled over and tried to sleep because I knew it would be morning soon.

MY BIG FIND

Stephen Bullock

I FOUND A HAND under a bench in the park when I was ten. A dead one. A human one. Burnt crisp and orange and hollow, with a three inch steel nail through the palm. I wondered if someone had been crucified. Or been tied to the railway line only to have a passenger train cleave all four extremities from the flailing body. I imagined the still twitching and bleeding hand bouncing down the embankment, finding its way to some local kids who proceeded to torture, burn and scream like toddlers at the grim article as they kicked and flicked it at each other. My imagination burnt so fiercely with the mystery of where this thing that should never, ever be found in a playpark could have appeared from, that there was no time for repulsion or horror. Finding a dead hand, as it turned out, was cool.

In truth it was the dog who found it, but I told the story different ways to different people for maximum impact. I quickly became a master storyteller, moving facts around and building tension through the details. Our dog, who I always fancied was the result of a happy union between a Jack Russell and a Rottweiler, had ferreted underneath one of the solid park benches and dragged something out. My mum launched herself at the dog, shouting 'Leave! Chas! Leave!' My mum had always wanted a King Charles spaniel but couldn't be doing with that much fur, so as the next best thing she bought a mongrel and called it Chas. It made sense at the time. We had been lectured again and again that Chas could die if he ate chicken bones as they have a tendency to splinter and a char-grilled chicken wing was the closest identifiable thing to what the dog now had between his saliva-drenched fangs. He was hoiked by his choke chain into mid-air, legs dangling, whining in utter desolation that his newfound tasty, beautiful plaything was lost to him. It wasn't chicken, but there were bones, rattling about inside the fried skin that was frozen in position with fingers bent but not clenched.

I managed to get a really good look at the dismembered hand, close enough to see the wrist bone jutting out from within the crispy-duck skin and the hacksaw grooves that had scarred the bone. Close enough to see the skin was almost transparent, and the fingerprints were still visible, like an amber resin model of the real thing. There was some screaming in my general direction and me and my brother were ordered away to a more respectable distance by my mum. I decided to set a good example to my six-year-old brother who was poking the thing with a stick. Poking a dead hand with a stick, as it turned out, was cool. I took the stick off him and we begrudgingly retreated to the steel safety of the big cube climbing frame.

I climbed to the very top where I had an aerial view of the body-less crime scene, drawing maps of the area in my head. A passing neighbour was sent scurrying home to telephone the police. That's what people did before mobiles, in the backward dark 80s. We formed a strange security team, guarding the hand from other dogs and passers by, shouting the news to gangs of kids from my lofty tower, like a medieval castle's gatekeeper – protecting my story until the police would take over. For a time we all felt terribly important.

The police came and cordoned the whole park off for several weeks as they searched it inch by inch. They even rang my mum and confirmed that the hand was really real, not fake. The relief washed over me, a bit like my grandma's tight knitted jumper going over my head. Having relished the story so far this was the best news. It was a genuine police-certified dead human hand. Fantastic. All too soon the tape came down and the police left with no new discoveries. They never found out whose hand it was, or even where it might have come from. Back in the playground tales of body snatchers, grave robbers, Mafia retribution and mislaid buckets of hospital amputations due for incineration were rife. I refused to pick an answer. I preferred the mystery. I told the tale to anyone who would listen, still do. I soon found myself part of an urban legend when a kid told me his best mate had found the hand in the park. I didn't correct him. After all, it was a great story.

That night my brother and I must have been suitably unaffected by the day as my parents went out for the night. My aunty Linda was nominated to babysit and being a responsible type she sent my brother to bed, but let me stay up to watch the Friday night horror film. It was called *The Hand*. Michael Caine's decapitated hand returns from the dead, strangles the cat, and finally tries to kill him too. I'm fairly sure I had a nightmare that night.

Although the hand was my first big story to tell, and probably nudged me into a career in storytelling and theatre, I don't believe the macabre nature of the dead hand I so vividly remember had any influence on my character. I am a happy, untroubled, married man who makes friends easily and runs a murder mystery theatre company. Basically I kill people for a living.

SPACE INVADERS

Sarah Macfarlane

MONDAY 8.43 a.m.

Our corner of the common room is Doc Martens, eyeliner and peroxide-blonde hair. And atmosphere. Yes, there's definitely atmosphere. I try not to angst but it seems it all intensifies when I sit down.

H concentrates on shuffling a pack of cards, A pulls at the edge of her too-short skirt, G pretends she's reading the dog-eared pages of her English homework, and L eats Space Invaders.

I sit it out.

I can't remember what I normally do to fill this time. It's not homework: I do that at home. It's not eating crisps: I've had muesli for breakfast. No, normally I talk to my friends about…well, stuff. Music, singers in bands, the weekend and the gig and how crap was the line-up and how much did we drink and who pulled who.

We will not be talking about that this morning.

Seventeen minutes tick by and I think about what I've done. Here it is: on Friday night, watching a crappy local band, I kissed D. The same D who dumped L the week before. After a lengthy relationship of 13 days. I've had plenty of time to think about my indiscretion, to be honest. All weekend. Reliving it is delicious.

PERIOD I

It's a relief to go to double maths with other kids who have muesli for breakfast and hand their homework in on time. I'm a straight-grades pupil so I spend a lot of time with kids like this. Kids who listen to bands like Texas, and shop in Next, and want to be doctors when they grow up. Today I don't mind, and I'm glad it's maths. I can arrange numbers without too much effort and switch to the part of my brain that's thinking of D. It's hard to be remorseful.

INTERVAL. COMMON ROOM

L's alone so I take the opportunity.

'Sorry about Friday. With D and everything.' I fix on my most sorrowful expression and don't say what I'm thinking, which is, get over him already, and, I would so do it again.

'I'm a total cow,' I add.

She smiles, all watery, and gives me a hug. We're friends again.

H arrives and deals me cards.

L munches on Space Invaders.

G bitches about Mrs T, English teacher from hell.

And I swear, A's skirt has got two inches shorter since this morning.

LUNCHTIME. I GO HOME

I watch TV, eat a balanced lunch, including fruit, and think about D.

He really is a good kisser.

I'm not a slut, I don't think, because I didn't go on Friday with the intention of pulling him. I didn't go with the intention of pulling anyone.

Well, not anyone in particular.

Think about it. I eat muesli but wear DMs. I listen to Smashing Pumpkins but still get straight grades. I can't afford to be fussy when it comes to boys.

I detour past Smokers' Corner where G and A have their token daily cigarette. And D too. I'm not going to lie. I want to see him.

There's no-one there. Only fifth year boys, hoping they look like Kurt Cobain when really they should invest in some Clearasil.

I don't think I'm needy, but if someone would just walk into the common room, sit down next to me and like me for me, even though I'm too clever and too healthy and much too rock...If someone did that...well, then I'd know, it's OK to be me.

COMMON ROOM

Space Invaders, 'On the Road', a random pair of DMs.

H is alone. 'There's been a crisis.' I roll my eyes. It's like we're living out *Reality Bites*, and it's not as thrilling as I would have expected. She deals me cards and we play. She's vicious and everyone returns as I concede a loss.

L's been crying.

A is supersolemn-faced.

G looks bored.

I don't say anything. I'm not convinced this newest catastrophe isn't about me so I wait till L and A go to geography. I have a free period.

G sits beside H and bursts open a packet of Space Invaders. They have maths but they won't go.

'What a drama.'

I try to read G's expression. She doesn't look like she hates me so I risk it, 'What happened?' 'Friday night, after you left, D got together with E. Her parents were away, and he went back to hers.' G shrugs. We all know what happens next.

I feel bad. Like, pain through my heart. Obviously D would pick E over me. She gets average grades, shops in Next, likes Texas, is overweight, bad hair, no sense of humour.

Good choice, huh?

I can't be upset about this.

Suddenly, H grins. 'For real? Has anyone seen D today? E didn't crush him to death?' I nearly giggle.

G chokes on Space Invaders.

'What is it with the overweight trendies? They get all the best guys.' 'We need to start eating more pies. Expand our waistlines.'

'E is easy, is all. Who hasn't she been with?'

'Still a waste,' I venture, then wait, see if I get more grief.

G smirks and I remember, she pulled D way back in December.

'God. He's such a he-slut.'

'Like J?'

'Totally. But not as cute.'

'You would know,' I state.

G looks smug.

H blushes.

I feel better.

We spend the afternoon pulling boys apart. It's all kind of satisfying, and I love these girls. Seriously. Because it doesn't matter that I'm good at maths and don't eat Space Invaders and think all Next franchises should be razed to the ground. It doesn't even matter that I kissed the wrong boy. These girls like me for me: Pearl-Jam-listening, straight-grades-achieving, misfit me.

And D. Seriously. To think I would have given this up for him.

'77 SUMMER OF SLAM

Martin McKay

1977 WAS A BIG YEAR, ask any punk or pottery collector. Punk had already reached the satellite towns around Glasgow for the big kids but if, like me, you were nine or ten then there was only one cultural watershed that summer. The big deal had four wheels and the sound, that sound – urethane rubber on concrete, ball-bearings rattling round – still makes my heart pound and I have to crane my neck to see. Summer '77, the skateboard had crash-landed. I was desperate but cash was tight.

Keith was a little younger than me and his auntie had a pair of old flyer senior roller skates in her shed. Together, we hatched the plot. One: get the skates, two: erm? Well, we'd figure out two later. Main thing was to get the skates.

Like a pair of Philadelphia lawyers, we charmed the birds out of the trees and the skates from his auntie.

The chancers now had to become skilled tradesmen. We had the necessary raw materials:

1   Rusty skates: two of,
2   Plank of wood: one of,
3   Nails: half inch (or half-inched!) and
4   the universal tool of all kids, the half brick.

Fool-proof, well-oiled, half-arsed, but we were ready to rock and roll!

We split the skates, cut the plank, battered and buckled the nails and eventually we had produced two (im)perfect, brick dust covered, classic examples of the world's greatest invention. I remember the day clearly, building the boards, all the while knowing we were in so much trouble for breaking the skates.

All we had to do now was ride them. The first steps, finding your feet or rather which foot went where. The wobble, the trapeze-like balancing act then: pain, skint knees, elbows, nose! I was scarred. I still am, but it was all good. It was summer, it was hot, it didn't rain; it never did, well except for the following year on the opening day of the World Cup, but that's another story. All

Keith and I knew was that a new world had opened up to us. We were rolling and falling and laughing.

And then came the hill. Between my home, in the flats, and Keith's house there was 'the lane'. This name did not adequately describe it. All year round it was there – quarter of a mile of slabbed concrete: scheme divider, young team boundary and in the winter the longest, fastest ice slide in the world. That summer brought the lane a new identity. It became the skateboard hill. It had never looked so steep. We had lived all our lives at either end of the lane but never had we viewed it with so much fear, respect and sheer delight. Ice was nice but c'mon!

There was a choice to be made before we took the great leap downward, however. Did we have the bottle to stand up or was it to be bum-boarding?

To my recollection, I took the hill like Ingmar Stenmark on Ski Sunday – and this is my story. Memory is your image of perfection as they say.

If I was still nine or 10 I would surely describe the feeling of skating down that hill in simple terms of joy and pure buzz. I am no longer 10, or 20, or even 30. Dude I'm 41 this year but that lane, that summer, if it was there I would have the exact same emotions well up. If I could stand at the top waiting to push off in to the total rush of it. Fast, scary and sore – heaven.

It's all gone now: the lane, my flats, the garages that you got chased off of by the polis for watching the downhill and slalom competitions. Keith's house is still there; his mum still lives in it. He is 40 this year and probably doesn't remember that summer in quite the same detail, I expect. So why do I?

Well, 30 years later you can't walk in my front door without tripping over several skateboards, at least one of which will be mine. My two boys have skateboards and my wife has kittens – regularly!

A BARGAIN SWAP

Paul Morris

I'D NEVER VISITED a castle before but we went, all of us, me and my big family to Culzean. I soon lost them and headed for the ramparts and there was the sea, angry with me, ramming the lower reaches of the walls below, dragged against its volition by a daytime, unseen moon. If you stood close to the edge there was no more castle, no more back there, no more me and my big family. There was out there.

And there was my purpose. As a boy, I never touched chocolate or sweets: instead I exchanged them for all manner of things. If you had two Mars bars and a Twix you were sought-after. Once the other kids had exhausted their stock of tooth massacre, they would sidle up to me and ask what I had in my pockets. I became the illicit owner of toy soldiers and cowboys and Indians that seemed too-melted in the manufacturing process, or the occasional kite, even sometimes an innocent-if-you-say-so peck on my quickly reddening cheeks from a girl whose sugar levels were out of control.

Today facing only the sea beyond Culzean, I held a toy parachutist in my hand, the best exchange so far by a million miles, a bargain swapped for a poke of scrap candy. I knew he was prepped for his virgin flight, folded parachute falling limply but correctly at his back. I had saved him for this and he was ready and I was ready: our moment. I barely paused and hurled him out there, sacrificing him to the turmoil of the wind and the inexplicable rage of the sea.

And he did not let me down. My guts rose to my throat as at first he plummeted but then the chute rose, flicker-flamed white and then opened. A joyous thermal took control and he floated off, so quickly, so perfectly that I wondered about the shortness of it. He was green but turned tiny-black as he punctuated the greyness – with enough white in it. Foul-mooded nature did not seem to affect him as he reduced himself to a dot and then absolutely nothing.

Me and my big family laid a tartan rug on the grass and it was invaded by picnic food, by bread and butter and ham and cheese and jam and marmalade and ginger (Cola and lemonade). We partook and, rightly so, there was a cathedral silence. Suddenly, he approached in the air behind us and I seemed to know he was coming. He landed near dead centre on the makeshift cloth table and lay there, green, too melted, silk tangled around his stiff legs.

MEMORABLE HOLIDAY

C. Edward Munyard

I FIRMLY BELIEVE that I was particularly fortunate with the parents I was born to, as they both felt there were two things of the utmost importance in the upbringing of their children. The first was that if history was being made, we should, if at all possible, somehow become involved. The second was to get away from London, where I spent my childhood, for an annual holiday, preferably by the sea. Occasionally, these two imperatives would coincide and then we had all the time in the world, or so it seemed, to observe history being made.

For several years we visited Southsea, a pleasant seaside resort near Portsmouth. I vaguely remember the narrow streets of small terraced houses fronted by the pavement, where we stayed with a lovely lady who just loved children and, consequently, spoiled us to bits.

According to Mum, she had one failing: if one admired any of her possessions small enough to be picked up, she would most certainly give it to you with an authoritative, 'You must have it then.'

'Now remember,' Mum would say, 'don't say you like anything unless it's your breakfast.'

Most of us treasure our possessions for the memories they evoke but Mrs Southsea got her pleasure from giving things away. Her 'You must have it' meant just that. There could be no argument. As a child, to find someone who would give you anything you asked for was oh so hard to resist, even with the constant reminders of 'Don't say you like anything,' ringing in your ears.

Being on holiday was so different to our usual routine. We would leave Mrs Southsea's house after breakfast and set off into town or to the sea front, wondering what the day had in store for us. But there was something special about this one day. We could tell we were going somewhere different by the knowing looks Mum and Dad gave each other, but where? And when? And, especially, why? Mum and Dad always made a game of such things and loved to keep us guessing.

At lunch we were warned, 'Don't make a pig of yourself. We don't want you being sick.' The question was why would we be

36

sick? This was answered as we made our way to the little pier where the boat trips were as Dad hurried us along with 'Don't want to be late.'

There was a queue at the pier by a big notice saying 'Trip around the Queen' in big bold letters. Brother Bob confirmed what it said, as my reading wasn't so hot. Well, I was only eight, I would complain when I couldn't do something.

'Why do we need a boat to see the Queen?' I thought as we were ushered onto the boat with the customary 'All aboard!'

'Which is the best side to stand?' Dad asked the man with the peaked cap.

'Won't matter, gov'ner,' said the man. 'The Queen's so big you can't miss her.'

We had been sailing for about ten minutes when all became clear. 'Here she comes,' the crowd seemed to say all together.

Somewhere, a man said 'Cor blimey!' Another, 'What a size!' A lady almost sung, 'How beautiful!' Everyone seemed most impressed, except me that is.

'Where's Mum?' 'Where's Dad?' I couldn't see anything. What were they all looking at? I was almost in tears as Dad came to the rescue. He swept me up in his arms and I was soon a 'flying angel' on his shoulders.

'Over there son' he said pointing west between the mainland and the Isle of Wight.

Then I saw it, smoke billowing from the funnels, the white bow wave breaking at the prow. What an amazing sight as the *Queen Mary* steamed toward us, slowly and majestically, everything about her gleaming and new, exactly as it should be for a Queen: for this Queen on her Maiden Voyage.

Today was 27 May 1936 and we were watching the *Queen Mary* as she steamed down the Solent on her maiden voyage to the United States of America and I was there with my family, once again privileged to see nautical history being made.

As the ship sailed closer, our tiny boat, a toy by comparison, bobbed about like cork. We came alongside at a safe distance where we could appreciate the enormity of this beautiful vessel. One can truly appreciate the size of the *Queen Mary* when looking up from sea level.

It seemed a never-ending wall of black and white, patterned by row upon row of portholes, and as she sailed by we could now look along her length. She was so long, in fact, one could not take her all in at one glance. She had to be almost read like a book.

I will never forget how small and insignificant our little boat seemed against this graceful giant, or what a tiny unimportant speck I was.

When our boat returned to the quay, we were amazed to find it moving up and down, by about one or two feet. It was like a ride at a funfair and it was taking a lot of timing for people to jump ashore.

I found it too difficult to even attempt and it was the man in the peaked cap who finally carried me ashore, no doubt kicking and screaming under his arm.

All this movement was, of course, caused by the wash of the Queen that arrived at the quay at the same time we did. The displacement of a ship of that size is enormous.

What an exciting finish to an amazing day for a boy of eight. I too was on the maiden voyage of the eighth year of my childhood. What a wonderful way to spend a birthday, a day remembered long after the birthday present I must have been given that day had been forgotten.

Thanks to mum and dad.

CATHARSIS IN THE CARROT FIELD

Grace Murray

YESTERDAY, I RAN away from home. The Rector had called me to his office. 'No!' he thundered, 'You may not have a week off school for swim training camp. Your marks are deplorable – especially maths and physics. If you don't do more work and less swimming, you may as well leave school right now!'

My heart plummeted. Swimming was the one thing I did better than my brilliant, beautiful big sister. I trained for four hours daily and hoped to get a place in the Commonwealth Games squad. That would make my parents like me.

The Rector glowered, waiting for a response. I snapped, 'Fine!' and stomped out. I tossed my schoolbag in a litterbin and hiked the eight miles to Glasgow. I had just enough money for a bus ticket to my grandmother's village in Fife.

Before approaching Granny, I called in at the local fruit farm where I'd worked the previous few summers. Mr Anderson was delighted to see me. He was desperately short-staffed and said I could start at five o'clock the following morning.

'I won't be a burden,' I assured my startled grandmother. 'I've got a job, and I'll help out in the house and garden.' She hugged me, and said I could stay as long as I wanted.

It was super at Granny's. She never compared me with my sister. There were fields behind her cottage and a brook in front, teeming with trout. Nearby were the woods and moorland I'd roamed so happily as a child. I would never go back to Paisley with its roaring traffic, sooty air and crowded tenements.

This morning began smoothly. The other seasonal workers are itinerants, barely literate and up to all sorts of tricks, so Mr Anderson had me supervising them – weighing and tallying their baskets of berries. We managed to get the 7.00 a.m. order off to Cupar market on time and Mr Anderson was pleased. He said he liked the way I'd handled the pickers and spotted their scams. He hinted that if I really wasn't going back to school, there might be a permanent job on the farm.

After a breakfast break, Mr Anderson set David, a neighbouring farmer's son and me to hand-weed a field of carrots. It was a horrible job – back-breaking and dirty. We could not have guessed that the farmer was testing us.

David and I worked alongside, in adjacent rows of the feathery green plantlets, but hardly spoke at first. I was shy of boys, self-conscious of my recent physical maturation and David was taciturn by nature.

Once we relaxed a bit, we discovered that we had much in common. We both loathed school, and both suffered from a dominant sibling – in David's case, an older brother who would inherit his family's farm.

We grilled in the shadeless field. Heat radiated from the parched earth and choking dust rose from every weed we shook. My perspiration-soaked hair dangled irritatingly. David noticed, and fished a length of twine from his pocket for me. I felt his eyes on my breasts as I lifted my arms to tie up my hair. We both blushed, and worked on in silence.

At the end of the next drill, David flung off his damp shirt and I found myself admiring his lithe, bronzed torso. He caught me looking. I blushed again, but he grinned.

To cover my confusion, I asked about his future plans and discovered that he too had just left school and was hoping for a full-time job here. I wondered guiltily if this could be the one Mr Anderson had just half-promised me.

David enquired in return about my plans and I confided how my ambition to be a teacher was ruined now I'd been expelled for too much swimming. He was interested in my training and we discussed that for a while, then David put his head on one side and asked, 'Isn't it boring, pounding up and down a pool?'

'Not really. I can think – and it feels good when you stop.'

'I'm a runner. It's nicer out of doors, and you get a buzz from that too.'

'I'd like to try.'

'I'll take you out one day.' We arranged a time and place.

When it was knocking off time, David went off home through the fields and Mr Anderson was waiting for me at the gate. He'd been watching us. He said my rows were good, still well cleared and firmed at the end of a long day. He'd noticed I'd had the initiative to stop and mend a hole in the rabbit fencing. The upshot was he offered me a job – proper training, with day-release to agricultural college. I asked to sleep on it.

'I'm home!' I carolled, then froze on Granny's threshold. My father was sitting at the kitchen table. Before I could bolt, he said, 'Sit down, pet, and listen to what we have arranged.' They had spoken to my coach and he said my selection was secure; I could ease back on the evening training sessions. The school wanted me back; I'd taken the Rector too literally. College admissions said I'd enough subjects already without maths and physics; I could drop those. 'So come home, sweetheart. We miss you so much.'

I looked down at my hands. I was no longer the petulant child who had fled yesterday. I felt valued and secure here with Granny. I'd given satisfaction at work and been offered a job with prospects. I'd formed a friendship with a boy and made a first date. David had made me realise that my obsessive swimming was pretty boring. It had been a desperate search for identity and acceptance – a crutch I didn't need any longer.

Two very different paths beckoned. Would I give up my new-found freedom and return to a life of dependency in town, or would I remain here in the country? It was decision time...

THE DAY THE WORLD FAILED TO END

Mark Palmer

9 JUNE 1985 was meant to be a momentous day in Earth's history. If the predictions were true however, there would be no-one left to scribble down a few notes about what happened. That's because the world was meant to end.

Except, it didn't.

Not a hint of trouble. It wisnae even slightly windy.

Myself and two friends had sat for most of the afternoon on the steps of the war memorial waiting for it to happen. At least, I think it was two friends. It may have been one. When the future of the world is at stake, the human mind can be selective about which facts it stores for later. It stands to reason. You've got to conserve brain space in case you need to remember the combination to disarm a bomb or such like which an evil mastermind has planted at the earth's core.

Sitting on the cold steps of the war memorial, I wasn't particularly sure how it would happen. Maybe it would be a huge fireball. Right there on the village green. Just in front of where the old boys from the British Legion lay their wreaths every year. Maybe an earthquake. I could picture a fireball more easily than an earthquake though. Being consumed by fire seemed somehow more 'end of the world' than falling into a crevasse.

Oddly enough, I somehow felt that if the world did end, Scotland would still be there. I had no difficulty imagining a Godzilla-like monster rampaging through Manhattan, ripping up buildings and swatting bi-planes. I could even stretch to a tidal wave washing Tokyo off the map. Somehow though, I couldn't imagine panic on the streets of East Lothian. Scotland would endure. Of that I was sure. The 14-year-old me just couldn't contemplate a world without Dougie Donnelly, Arthur Montford and *Weir's Way*.

Let's face it. If anyone survived, they would need some cultural icons. 'Up go the heads' and all that.

As I sit here in 2008, the internet reveals that the end of the world in 1985 was meant to be caused by Armageddon starting in 'a valley on the Alaska Peninsula'. All a bit vague. At the time I didn't really give much consideration to exactly why the world would end or whose fault it was. That was easy. Like any Scottish child of the 80s, I blamed Maggie Thatcher.

After all, anyone evil enough to steal school kids' milk was a snap for starting a world ending conflict.

About two and a half hours passed and nothing happened. Not a fireball. Not even a spark. Stomachs rumbled. A shuffling of feet occurred as the observers of the world's demise started to wonder what was for their tea.

It was probably chips. Was it not always something with chips in the 1980s? In many ways, a good plate of egg and chips would have been an entirely satisfactory foundation upon which a boy could face oblivion.

Like any group of 14-year-olds awaiting the end of the world, there was a tough decision to be made. Was the end of the world really going to be spectacular enough to justify a hiding from your ma for being late for your tea.

'I'll come in for you efter ma dinner then'.

'Aye.'

We walked away from the war memorial. By the time tea was served, the world had still not ended.

By the time I'd had my pudding I'd forgotten all about Armageddon.

SECRETS, LIES AND GRANDAD

Elaine Renton

I REMEMBER THE DAY Grandad asked me. 'Have you told anyone?'

I answered. 'No.'

Lying was easy after that.

Grandad slid his hands onto his knees and leaned down until his face was at my level. He smelt of Old Spice and Capstan Full Strength and he had missed a bit on his chin when he was shaving.

'I'm going to show you something,' he said, 'a special thing that you must keep a secret. All right?'

I nodded, trying to keep the fizz of excitement from getting the better of me.

Grandad winked at me and said with a voice full of smiles, 'Come on then.'

We walked down to the far end of the garden where Grandad had a heap of gardening rubbish ready for burning. A male blackbird followed us, dipping and swooping and giving a constant chook of alarm. We stopped at the tangle of hawthorn branches and last year's weeds and the blackie settled in the rowan tree. He dipped his tail feathers and released some droppings before continuing with his strident call. I could see that his eyes were ringed with white.

Grandad carefully moved aside a cut branch. 'Now, you stand here in front of me and don't say a word.'

I did as I was told and held my breath just in case a word escaped.

'Mrs Blackbird's decided to raise her family here.' Grandad spoke softly in my ear. 'Isn't that nice?'

I peered through the dried branches and brittle leaves and there was the mother bird, fluffed up and unconcerned by her visitors. She was hidden well back in the bonfire, sitting on an untidy nest made of twigs.

'She's laid three eggs.' Grandad said. 'And she's lined the nest with soft grass to keep them safe. Clever eh?'

The blackbird half closed her eyes and gave a little nod as if agreeing with my Grandad.

'I've been watching her for a couple of days and she doesn't mind a wee visit now and then.' Grandad replaced the branch. 'Now away you go and remember, no telling.'

I know now that information is power but back then my six-year-old self couldn't get away fast enough to tell the boys on the farm. I was jubilant. I wanted a go on their bikes and now I had something to bargain with. Grandad went back into the cottage and of course I belted across the road and right into the farmyard.

The three brothers were tinkering with their bikes as usual and I had never felt so important in my short life.

'Guess what?' I asked but continued without waiting to see if they could guess what 'what' was. 'A blackbird has made a nest down by the rowan tree at the bottom of our garden. My Grandad said that she's sitting on three eggs.'

I did my nervous thing of reaching around and easing my shorts out of my bum. 'Can I get a shot of the red bike?'

The brothers looked at each other. One of them edged a bike towards me using the toe of his wellie. It was the oldest bike, yellow, and far too big for me. I pulled it up and tilted it over until it was low enough for me to swing my leg over the bar.

My feet barely reached the pedals so I stood on tiptoe and wobbled out onto the road and away. The hedgerows rushed past me in a blur as I pedalled on. After a mile or so I made an uncertain turn on the brow of a hill then sped back home standing on the pedals. Evening midges battered my face so I closed my eyes. The bike veered and hit the grass verge and I was sent sprawling onto the warm tarmac while the yellow bike continued solo for a few yards before crashing too.

In the distance I heard the male blackie's call of alarm then a bird flew over me in frantic flight. I knew from the flash of pale throat and the dark speckled plumage underneath that it was a mother blackbird. I sat up and looked at the raw scrapes on my knees and palms and felt sick.

The youngest brother came down our path. He stopped, looking closely at my oozing grazes.

'Ouch,' he said without any real sympathy, 'look what I've got. More for our collection. We've got loads in an old drawer under my bed.'

He held out three greeny-blue eggs. The light, glossy surfaces were sprinkled with reddish spots. I knew that these fragile things should be back in the soft lining of their untidy nest.

'I'm away to have a bash at blowing them.' He hoisted up the battered bike with his free hand. 'I'll find my mum. She'll have a look at your knees.'

Putting the eggs in a drawer sounded safe enough so I sat with stooning knees, occasionally licking my rusty blood and spitting out bits of gravel.

The farmer's wife finally came out of the yard wiping her hands on a tea towel.

'You've had a fall then? Come on, let's get you sorted before your Grandad sees you.' She helped me up and led me into the scullery. 'Here, hold your hands under the cold tap and I'll find the Germoline.'

Three eggs lay puddled in the plughole of the cracked porcelain sink. The yolks were flecked with blood and on the windowsill an old rag lay beside pot scourers and a soap dish. Nestled on the rag and far from the safety of their soft nest were three blackbird's eggs. They were neatly pierced at both ends and drying in the sun and I vomited bile, the same colour of yellow as the yolks.

After that, my idea of a secret was to tell everyone in a whisper.

1971

Susan Stewart

'IS IT WHERE the sweet shop is?'

'No. It's just after Easter Road, mind?'

'Is it after the big trees?'

'No, before the trees. Susan, ye ken where it is, you do.'

It was 1971. It was winter, and this was my Mum trying to get me to make a doctor's appointment on my own. I was eight.

I wasn't bothered about going to the doctor's. I'd been there loads. You had to tell the big lady with the horn rimmed glasses you'd arrived, and then sit in the massive waiting room where the gnarly old wooden table dominated the entire space. You got to sit in one of the huge leather couches that smelt of...well, leather actually, but I didn't know that then. You didn't speak to anyone and if you said anything at all, you had to whisper. Fine by me.

Nowadays, you wouldn't dream of sending your average eight-year-old out to the shops without a serious amount of counselling for the bairn afterwards. But, as a single parent of eight years, my mum had to force me into such angst-ridden tasks to save time and yes, probably her job. Did her boss even know she had children? Possibly not. Of course, the downside of these sparkling solutions was having to convince me that I had the ability to survive such a trial. Obviously she had a faith in me that I couldn't quite grasp yet.

As the youngest, I often had my older brother as my guide. He was 12, and he did all my thinking for me. But he was somewhere else on that day, and this meant me having to do it myself.

'How can you no' take me?'

'Because I've had too much time off my work. It was the only appointment they had, so, I need to meet you there. You'll only be about 10 minutes before me.'

She'd taken many jobs over the years. Manual labour, factory work, office work, bookie's assistant, anything nine to fiveish would do. Oh, and an early morning cleaning job if she was saving up for something. Anyway, things were looking up because we were emigrating to New Zealand and once we'd jumped through all the hoops they'd amassed for us, we'd be flying off to better things. Goodbye to wintry, cold, flea-bitten Scotland and all who lived in her.

We had to do interviews, get references and endure several medicals and do things like pee in a measuring jug for urine samples. Always a novelty. And I so wanted to go to New Zealand. I was absolutely clueless as to what to expect from such a place. I had to rely on school maps, and Mum's snippets of life in a city called Dunedin, furnished by her own sister who had settled there five years earlier. But we'd once watched an Elvis movie together, and she'd said we were going to a place like that. I'd gazed with an envious eye at the people in that film. They looked happy, and they sang and danced, and they wore grass skirts and the sun shone. Great!

As it turned out, she managed to get away from work early. My instructions were to meet her at the bus stop on Craigentinny Road. She'd already be on the bus, and I was to be there a 4.30 p.m.

That was the wee hand between the four and the five, and the big hand on the six. And the bus fare was under the clock. Oh, and I had to mind to lock the door...and put the key in my zippy pocket, because if I lost it...

She was on the top deck, front seat – my favourite. She stood up to her full 4ft 11 inches so I could see her, and I stumbled onto the bus and up the stairs at full pelt. As we journeyed past the council houses and further on to Jock's Lodge, the heavens opened and the rain battered down onto the top of the bus. How grateful I was, at that moment, that I wasn't on my own. That I had my lovely Mum sitting beside me, watching the rain make the locals scurry and sprint for cover in the gloom of the early evening. That we were dry and warm in that damp smelling, smoky top deck, heading into Edinburgh.

Lost in a monologue about something important to me, I noticed we were approaching our stop. I slipped off the seat and only then realised Mum was resting a steady gaze on me.

'What are you getting up for?' she asked quietly.

My head swivelled in my attempts to orientate myself.

'So, ye kent which stop to get off at after all, eh? she said. 'You're no' as daft as yer cabbage lookin, Susan.'

I took that as a compliment.

THE SPRAY BATHS

Donald Wilson

I JUST COULDN'T SLEEP. Tomorrow was the big day. My mind tried to imagine what to expect of the spray baths. Here I was in primary one at Shakespeare School. On my first day it took three teachers to manhandle me in through the doors kicking and screaming and then not a week later when I asked old Mrs Wilson if I could go to the toilet, she sent me back to my seat petrified so much that I peed myself sitting on my chair. What on earth were they putting me through now? I just needed to sleep and maybe it would all be just a bad dream.

'Have you got your towel?' said my mum.

'Aye' I said as I rolled up the rough bristly towel like a Swiss roll.

'Now just enjoy your spray bath.'

Oh no those words again!

The walk to school was like a walk to the gallows and I played a game of giant steps and baby steps in my mind, only I was taking baby steps all the way. Soon enough I was there at the gates. Here goes, I thought. My hands and fingers twisting and turning as I tried to squeeze the nerves out and leave them behind in the playground. I went through the big doors.

'Stand up, boys and girls.'

'Let's say the Lord's Prayer...Our Father who art in heaven.'

'I wish I was in heaven.' I prayed.

'Amen,' said the teacher. I was still in the class, the Lord had forsaken me.

There was a knock at the door and in walked two big women in pinnies. They looked like twins. Big bosoms, big arms and kindly faces. They looked like big aunties that would hug you until you couldn't breathe.

I didn't catch their names but I did catch the last part 'will take all the boys for your spray bath, please remember your towels'.

I grabbed hold of my Swiss roll towel and joined the queue.

'This way, boys.'

They led us downstairs next to the Jannie's office.

'Don't forget to gie them some Lifebuoy,' laughed the Jannie.

We were led into a big open room that had wooden benches all around it. The windows were frosted and the bright sunshine shone through.

'Right, boys, take aff yer stuff and put them in a pile oan the bench and hing yer towel oan the peg.'

We all scampered to a space and began to take off our clothes. I did this facing the wall. I didn't want to look at anyone else and I didn't want anyone looking at me. The Y-Fronts were still on and I turned my head around.

'All of your clothes boys, even yer YS'

I slid mine down and put them on my pile.

There was a sudden noise from the room across from us. Gushing water.

'Right, boys, this way.'

We all walked forward like little naked penguins.

The room was filling with steam and I could make out pipes on the walls which went upwards and then turned to face the ground with what looked like the end of a watering can. There was hot water raining out of these spouts.

'Right, boys, get yerselves under a spray and grab some soap.'

We all made haste to the sprays. There were whoops and shrieks as the boys each got under the hot steamy water. The first thing I did when I got to mine was to raise my hands palms outward and feel the heat and comfort of the water. This was terrific. I shut my eyes and let the water pour over my head, through my hair and snake its way down my back, giving me goose bumps as it went.

I picked up my soap and lathered it in my hands. It smelled great. I rubbed it all over. I was standing there like a big bubbly Michelin Man. The water swirled at my feet as we all stood in a trench that collected the water and sent it running towards a drain in the corner. I squatted down and cupped a hand full of water. What else could I do with this but throw it to the boy next to me. 'Hoy, chuck it, you!' he squatted and cupped his hands in the water. Whoosh, over it came. This was catching on and the noise of the boys was louder that the sprays.

'Right, boys, that's enough.'

'Start tae rinse yerselves.'

'Pit the soap doon.'

Our two big aunties were in the centre of the room and now letting us know that our time in the sprays was coming to an end.

'Right, boys, oot ye come, time tae dry yerselves.'

After all I had been through there was no way I was leaving this aquatic playground.

A few boys had started to shuffle back to their piles and started drying themselves.

Me and a couple of others just stood there under the sprays. We were obviously the ones that had a bath in the sink because we stayed in a room and kitchen.

'Right, boys, Ah'm no kiddin.'

Still no movement.

'OK, yer gonny get it.'

We all looked at each other, what were they going to do, come and drag us out?

I saw one of the Aunties adjust something on the wall.

'WAAAAAAAAAAAAAAAAAAA,' the shrieks came simultaneously.

The nice hot stream of water had suddenly turned to freezing cold needles that were stabbing at our bodies. I made a hasty slippery getaway towards my pile.

'BRRRRRRR,' I did not realise that I had said that out loud but that was the noise I made as I unrolled the Swiss roll and began trying to dry myself.

In no time I was dressed and back at my desk poking my finger into my ear to try and let the water out. All that fuss and the spray baths were the best things in school ever! My nerves were well and truly cleansed.

A MOVING STORY

James Wrethman

WHEN I REACHED the summer of my 11th year I was hit by a bomb-shell: we were moving out of Govan. The new apartment would be in Penilee, a housing scheme originally built to accommodate the workers of the nearby Hillington Industrial Estate.

My parents saw this move as a great opportunity, for although it was still a council property, we would have a living room, kitchen, two bedrooms and wonder of wonders, a bathroom and toilet to ourselves – inside the apartment.

However, at that time no amount of salesmanship by my parents could convince me that this was a desirable move. Likewise, no amount of tears and tantrums could convince them that I would be better staying in the back courts of Rathlin Street where I could climb the dykes, catch giant beetles and throw slates at the rats which populated the 'middens'.

The trauma I was going through lasted until the removal men invited me to travel inside the van with them as they made their way to our new home. The novelty and excitement of the 'flittin' (house-moving in Glaswegian) overcame my sadness at leaving, and fear of the unknown.

The first school I attended, after our move from Govan to Penilee, was Linburn Primary, a one-storey construction which formed a quadrangle on a large open field in the centre of the housing scheme. One event in particular was to mark the start of my educational experience at Linburn. I call it my 'hubris' moment – a rapid descent from a momentary high.

The school perimeter was marked by a six-foot-high iron fence. In those days, it was probably there to keep pupils in; today, such a barrier's main purpose might well be to keep maniacs out. The height was no doubt deemed sufficient to deter ten-year-old or younger pupils from absconding during playtime. It was unfortunately not high enough, to stop my left-foot (meant only for standing on) shot. Instead of the ball rebounding gloriously from between the two jackets hanging there to mark the goal, it infuriatingly and agonisingly ballooned over the barrier and into the waste ground beyond.

Missing a golden opportunity in front of goal is enough to make you unpopular with your own side. Losing the only ball over the fence attracted unanimous displeasure. There was only one way to retrieve the situation and here my earlier Govan dyke-climbing experiences could be put to good advantage. I hauled myself up on to the perpendicular bar which joined the rails about one foot from the top and perched there with my feet lodged between the spiked-tops. I paused to select a place on which a short-trousered schoolboy could safely land, on waste ground almost entirely covered by tall nettles. I also lingered for effect. I was sure not many of the guys and certainly none of the girls, who I hoped were now watching, would have been able to perform such a feat. Satisfied, that I was now the centre of attention I sprang forward and downwards from my perch. There seemed to be a momentary resistance but the gravitational pull carried me through it and I landed safely, if a little clumsily. But the momentary resistance I had overcome, drooped on the fence like a flag at half-mast: my shorts.

Much later I would reflect that the situation could have been worse. The trouser leg which had snared on the spike could have held, instead of giving way at the seams. In which case, I would have been left dangling ridiculously from the fence and would have required assistance to get down. But, at that moment, amid the laughter emanating from the other side of the fence, I could find no immediate consolation. Neither would I quickly retrieve the situation. Boys being boys, my trousers were gleefully seized and were now being paraded around the playground to maximise my embarrassment.

I was now obliged to re-scale the fence as the only other alternative was to walk round to the street entrance, in my underpants, and ask for admittance from the Janitor. This option I did not find immediately appealing. Apart from the fact that, once again, I would look ridiculous, I'd have to admit to breaking the rules on leaving the school grounds and that would put me in deep trouble with the Head.

Before starting the ascent I did try unsuccessfully to barter the ball for my trousers, in the vain hope that when I did get over I could somehow salvage some pride by wrapping them around me. But now the sound of the assembly bell, to mark the end of playtime, made my return to the other side all the more urgent.

Unfortunately, a dip in the ground on the waste-land side, and clumps of barbed weeds and nettles, made the climb from the outside a much more formidable task. Haste does not aid precision. Several shin bruises and nettle-stings later I was finally able to land on the other side. Just in time to arrive trouser-less and red-faced to the centre of the playground, where the now massed ranks of sniggering and guffawing pupils were only just being kept under control by several teachers who awaited my explanation with interest.

I was punished, sent home with borrowed pants and a note describing my disgraceful conduct. My parents said the event only served to reinforce the points they had been making for some time.

Dad: that I should practise more with my left foot.

Mum: that I must always wear spotlessly clean underwear.

Love and Family

MOVING ON

(anonymous)

MY ALARM CLOCK, in the form of the builder's digger, wakes me, as usual half an hour too soon. And as usual I turn over and try to snatch an extra few minutes' sleep. As usual it doesn't work. A normal day. Except.

Except that today the two little people who have lived with me for so long are 'moving on' – to a permanent foster placement where they will stay until they are independent. Every day since we were told of the plan I have prayed that it will be a 'moving on'. I hope so, for they don't need more trauma, more loss.

It is 7.00 a.m. and they will not go to school today. There are three and a half hours left before their new carers will come for them. Three and a half hours of 'last' things.

The last time that the little one will climb onto the top of my bed clutching a handful of cars that he will run up and down on the cover, broom-brooming, on the hills I make of my legs.

The last breakfast. Unusually quiet, with only my husband managing his normal one Weetabix and a slice of toast. Today there is no 'you can't leave until you've finished or you'll lose your play-piece' rule.

The last gathering up of toothbrushes and pyjamas and all the needed things that must wait until the end.

The last searching behind chairs and under cupboards for things that otherwise might be left.

The last bounce on the trampoline, the last playing 'passies' with the football, that I video because she has asked that I make a memory for me to keep.

We have bought small gifts for them. One fails to work, the other is instantly broken, perhaps deliberately, and so we have a last trip to the pocket money shop and both make a new choice.

The suitcases stand in the hall and because I know that if I have to keep looking at them I will cry, we go out to 'our' coffee shop. This time they have a free choice of all the cakes.

When we come back I take them one at a time and we look through their photo albums, remembering the good times, trying to

57

laugh together. The post comes, cards and good wishes from our extended family. He rips his open, hugs the pictures to him, while she focuses on the messages, touching each gently.

Their 'goodbyes' in our street have already been said – in a tea-party that they handled much better than I had expected – but today there is the last ride up and down on their bikes, the last stopping to speak to those who have been surrogate grandparents to them.

I am in the kitchen, wrapping their special cups, when she flies in to tell me it is 10.30 a.m. and wraps her arms around me in a fierce hug. That is our real goodbye, for when the car comes we concentrate on loading it up and when it is done she climbs in and drops her head. 'We will see you', I say (for we are to keep some form of contact, though not soon) but my voice breaks as I strap her brother into his seat and I shut the door quickly. He stares out at us, bewilderment clear in his face. She doesn't look up. Nothing in all the careful preparations has equipped any of us for this last moment.

We force ourselves to stay standing by the edge of the road, in case either of them should look back, but I cannot see anything and so don't know when the car has disappeared around the corner. And then, uncharacteristically, my husband suggests shopping.

THE FLAT ON THE ROUNDABOUT

Rachel Ashe

THERE'S TEARS COLLECTING in my ears. I smile through my moment of despair and turn to you in bed and say, 'I have puddles in my ears; there are tears in my ears'. You laugh in a sad way and look at me adoringly. 'You should write a poem, babe.'

'I'm going to – there are tears in my ears will be the first line, perhaps it can be added to the poem – this lift stinks like piss.'

You laugh again and squeeze my hand and pull me in close. Your eyes have gone all bleary again and the puddles in my ears feel as if they are overflowing.

'We're not very good at saying goodbye are we? We always end up having too much fun. Perhaps this is why we haven't actually managed the leaving each other bit yet. Perhaps sixth time lucky, aye?'

You smile and squeeze my hand again in agreement.

I'm thinking how strange to feel so sad yet also kind of be enjoying the closeness of a goodbye. All the best things are said at the end.

I look up and realise that the day is almost over; orange glow comes through the window and kisses the wall behind your head. I turn to the light and screw up my eyes and shiny stars and sparks dance through my eyelashes.

The room smells warm. Your breath smells like whisky and sleep; I sniff the skin on the inside of my arm – Radox and Nivea. I think about how earlier you breathed me in while you had your eyes closed and sighed happily.

'I love your smell. You always smell clean.'

You're dozing off now, your eyes are puffy and red; I know my eyes are swollen too. I stare intently at your face, trying to memorise every detail, every tiny hair and every tiny freckle.

I can't quite believe it's been over two years since I put that scrap of paper under your door declaring my love to you. How embarrassing of me. You always say that I work in fast forward whereas you're usually stuck on pause.

I pinch your nose between my thumb and forefinger and you wake with a start.

I can tell I look determined because you make an effort to wake up and pay attention.

I know this face so well. It knows me too.

There's a film playing in my head to an old song. Our happy faces dancing across my mind. At least a hundred memories of you, but the one that sticks is you grabbing my foot unexpectedly and holding it while we watched a film two years ago. It felt so sweet. So precious a memory. I banked it right there and then – a moment for later. I suddenly wonder what the film was.

I take a breath and cross my fingers on the hand which isn't in your grasp and pluck up courage to ask the question one last time.

'Are you sure? You're sure you don't love me. That you never did, you just see me as a friend?'

You look sad and nod your head.

I release my hand from yours and push your body away from my own and roll to the other side of the bed and let the space between us grow.

BLACKBERRIES, BUTTERFLY WINGS AND MINSKY MOMENTS

Patricia Byrne

HER RECIPE COLLECTION is on my kitchen table, held together in a sheet of folded cardboard tied with a thick, black elastic band. She had sellotaped notes on the folder cover: ingredients for festive mince pies, ginger-bread, and beetroot with apple and red jelly. Inside, she had used odd pieces of paper to write her recipe details – curry sauce ingredients on the inside of a Christmas card page; red biro writing on fragments of a bank document giving details of an Easy Lemon Cake. And then there are the glossy leaflets she had collected – Woman's Own Guide to Success with Cakes and Pastries; Supervalu Sweet Stacked Pancake Sensation; the McDonnell Good Food Kitchen guide: I bake it better with Stork.

In the middle of this bounty of food ingredients, I had come upon smudged ink notes for a mixture of methylated spirits, linseed oil and turpentine to be used for removing furniture marks.

The hand-written notes for 'Nine Flighty Butterflies from One Easy Recipe' had started us off as children on our cooking careers. Now, I feel again the thrill of slicing the tops of freshly-baked buns, cutting the butterfly wings from the sponge pieces and placing them triumphantly on top of thick, whipped cream.

But it was jam-making that really took my mother's fancy. I thumb through more than a dozen pages of step-by-step jam-making instructions for bramble apple, blackberry, gooseberry, raspberry and autumn-medley mixtures. The pages are stained and smudged but I am glad that I rescued this bundle of sheets from the empty house after her death.

This morning I lowered the blind in the front window against the yellow autumn light that speckled the brown edges of the leaves on the horse chestnut tree outside. It is a day for fruit-picking. The recipes, jars and ingredients are ready. I do a whirlwind tour of the house and put away clothes in a back-bedroom wardrobe, a room long vacated by my now grown-up and departed son. My eyes are drawn to the cherry-red framed picture on the wall at the head of the bed, a rare display of artistic talent by my first-born, it is a child's drawing of an autumn scene: three large, brown horse-chestnut leaves stuck at random across the picture. Each leaf is outlined with bright red paint, the colour chosen when the picture was brought proudly to be framed. Two painted figures, with a dog nearby, appear to leap and dance above the ground among the swirling leaves. As they jump, they lift their arms toward the blue sky above them. There is a house in the distance. I marvel at my son's untutored strokes, capturing the magic of child's autumn dance under a blue sky. Now, in my mind, I see a group of children under the horse chestnut tree in the front, heaping conkers into a small wheelbarrow and piling them beside the garden shed in the back.

House chores finished, I set off to gather blackberries by the estuary. I kick golden rattling leaves, stoop to pick a prickly horse chestnut capsule which is starting to split open, like a crab shell, to reveal twin conkers side by side in a milk-white bed. I search out the blackberries in the hedges, scratch my arms with thorns, and feel nettle scotches on my legs. I reach for bundles of ripened berries which fall into the container with a mere shake of the branch. I stuff soft berries into my mouth, my fingers purple-stained from the juices. Later, I prepare the fruit, remove the stalks, take away any under-ripe berries and simmer them with water and lemon juice, add sugar, then rapid-boil the purple-black mixture.

The evening news on the radio is filled again with credit crunch stories and turbulence on financial markets. A man is explaining about a Minsky moment – which gets its name from the now deceased American economist, Hyman Minsky. I am trying hard to understand what the man on the radio is saying. It seems that a Minsky moment happens when investors take on so much risk that the returns they make are no longer enough to service their debts. When this happens, lenders call in their loans and investors are forced into a fire sale of their assets. Hard times are here again. We haven't had it so bad since the 1929 Depression. On the radio, they debate about how long the economy will stay in the doldrums.

I fold my mother's recipe notes; put them back into the cardboard folder that holds her finger prints; think of her setting out jam jars on a kitchen table in a yellow pebble-dash bungalow; imagine myself running from school through crackling leaves with the tastes of hot blackberry pie and thick custard on my tongue.

My son phones. Life is stressful, millions are being lost: he is worried about compliance issues. Lehman Brothers have gone to the wall. How could this happen? He has never heard of anything like this before. I listen to him, offer encouragement. A funny thought occurs to me: I feel like asking if he has walked through fallen autumn leaves or picked conkers this year. But I don't say this; it wouldn't be well received. I tell him to look after himself, get a good night's sleep, eat properly.

The blackberry jam is setting nicely in an assortment of jars on my kitchen table. The evening sun is now low in the sky, no longer shedding light on split conkers under the tree in the front garden. A child who once danced among autumn leaves has grown into a young man stressed by the turbulence of financial markets. I am happy that today I opened once more my late mother's recipe folder and set out on the annual ritual of folding the fruits of autumn into winter sustenance.

LOVE KNOTS

Elizabeth Clark

WE MANAGED TO GET them the best room in the place. The twin room had en suite facilities and big bright windows, overlooking the forests and glens we'd explored with Grandpa when we were young. He and Granny loved Dundonald Woods, maybe even walked in them together when they were courting. There were tales of bluebells as high as my daddy, deep dark pools of frogspawn and sausage sizzles with brownies and boy scouts. Happy days.

These days, life moved at a slower pace for Granny and Grandpa, confined to the care home, wistful, tired and a little bemused at how it had come to this. They stood proudly at the head of a family of two children, four grandchildren and, at that point, three great-grandchildren and another on the way.

On one of my last ever visits to Dundonald House, I found Granny and Grandpa in the day room. Nothing much happened there, but it was a change of scene from their own room and there was the chance that someone new might strike up a conversation. They were seated side by side watching television and in their hands were the opposite ends of my Grandpa's handkerchief. He always carried one in his pocket. I remembered him clearing the windscreen of the car with it on our many trips around Scotland, turning it into his silly hat on the beach at Girvan, wiping away my childhood tears.

But in the care home, there were no dirty windscreens, no sunny beaches and no crying children. What remained was a deaf old man and an old lady whose eyes had ceased to see. When I asked about the hanky, my Grandpa said it was their love knots. If Granny needed anything, all she had to do was pull on her knot and Grandpa would sort it out. It's just as well Granny had gone blind and Grandpa was distracted by the football on TV. Neither of them saw the tears streaming down my cheeks.

Granny died on the Friday. When I visited Grandpa the next morning, he said he was going to be with her. By the following Friday he was gone. After 67 years of marriage, no love knots were strong enough to mend his broken heart.

AUTOPSY

Miranda Doyle

Irvine Welsh's favourite story

I DECIDE I WANT to see what is left of my father.

His brain lies in Glasgow's Southern General Neuropathology Department, donated to science in 2002. He died of a fast growing brain cancer. A tumour wove insidiously through the folds of cortex above his left ear. It became enmeshed with his synapses, flowering like deceit.

Professor Graham, who cut his brain from its stem, has asked me to go straight up to the Neuropathology Department on the fifth floor.

It is on the first floor where men in blue scrubs, like this one, belting a vending machine, excavate brains from the living. And it is on the fifth, where another band of doctors excavate them from the dead.

I press five on the button panel where once I had pressed six. Then, when Dad was alive, I shuddered upwards in the lift. His ward was reached past a crayoned picture of Winnie the Pooh on the closed door of the children's room, and a pen for families awaiting news. He often sat by the window, his stapled skull nodding against his chest in sleep.

The lift opens onto floor five. There are scarred wooden double doors and the smell of the laboratory. Professor Graham gets up to shake my hand. In his office we sit down opposite one another, and I say, 'Where does it live?'

The question is out of me before I can think of something more sensible to ask.

Professor Graham rises from his chair and walks across the corridor to another room. He returns with a shallow plastic bucket in white, informing me that the donation had started out in a larger one. The consistency of the brain is like jelly, he tells me, and very difficult to work with. And it was in the larger bucket that the material, as he calls it, was fixed. And once hard, what was left of my father was cut into 14 pieces.

He leans over and points out a book, lying open next to me on the desk.

I look. The photograph is black and white, and shows a full brain sliced and arranged, left to right. Perhaps, I think, it will be less gruesome to view in pieces, than as a bulk of creases and folds; recognizable as a brain. And as something that was once his. In my anxiety at what must come I tear on, saying: 'I wondered why his testes were not examined in the autopsy. I wondered whether it was a kind of man to man thing, that you left this part of him alone as a mark of respect.'

Professor Graham looks at me blankly. I repeat the question.

'The post mortem report states that the testes were not examined.'

He rises, and this is the only moment the whole afternoon where he looks flustered, reaching over his desk for the post mortem report. Carefully he turns the page and apologises. It is an oversight, he says, asking if I am worried that the cancer had spread.

'No, I am not worried about the cancer,' I tell him. 'It was only that it seemed a glaring omission. Unbeknownst to me my father was unfaithful to my mother the whole of their married lives.'

And so typical, I think to myself, that his testes should defy that damning autopsy label that had defined each of his other organs – 'unremarkable'.

But the brain is not now in its bucket, I am told. Professor Graham informs me that the viewing of the remains has been arranged downstairs in the mortuary chapel.

In the lift, once the doors have concertinaed closed, he says cheerily to another doctor: 'This young lady has come to discuss a donation her family have made to the department.'

The man colours and the exchange gives me the feeling that in all his years as a pathologist, and he is due for retirement in a month, Professor Graham has never experienced a mission like this.

Outside the rain has stopped. At the mortuary we ring the bell. A shadow hobbles into view. Mr Scott has a stick. Professor Graham tells me that Mr Scott has hurt his back and Mr Scott, in white coat and blue scrubs, nods.

We enter the chapel, and again Professor Graham reassures me that I may not want to see it. But there is nothing that would make me turn back now.

Mr Scott opens the door to the viewing chamber. There is a small room with no chairs, a glass panel in one wall. The window is curtained. Behind it appears a hospital trolley-bed pushed up beneath the glass. Covered in white linen, it carries the brain.

The sections are in three rows on a white tray. Dad's label is soaked and almost unreadable with its autopsy name, number and place of death: Doyle AO30139: Ayrshire Hospice.

The tissue itself is in two shades of beige. Grey and white matter has been fixed to colours never chosen in the Dulux palette. The slices increase in size from the prefrontal section through to the diced gristle of the brain stem. The seventh slice has a small hole, the eighth a larger one, whilst the ninth and tenth show ragged edges. The cavity is enormous.

The men wait for me to speak. It is impossible to imagine that this is him, that who Dad was, and who he pretended he wasn't, collided against the fan of nerve endings, which are as clear as the roots of a tree.

I begin asking questions about the cavity and the discolouration, but I no longer care what the answers are.

That I am in this room feels like another autopsy. One in which I should emulate Professor Graham. He has retained cassette-sized sections of what was healthy to store beside what was diseased. He remained impartial in the face of a rampant brain tumour.

He accepted my father as he was.

MIBBLY

Stewart Ennis

THE WEATHER WAS PERFECT. I'd wanted to do this trip with her for a while but things got in the way. She was too young to appreciate it, or days put aside were spoiled by poor weather. Also, I didn't want our nostalgic cycle trip into Daddy's childhood to turn into an endurance test. But the tag-a-long bike, that converted my bike into a tandem, had made it possible. She loved it; and even though she was only six she could really help propel us along. In fact sometimes on the flat, I would put my feet up and let her do the pedalling.

'Daddy! I'm doing all the work.'

We took the bikes by train into Paisley and found the cycle track that led to Bridge of Weir. 'This used to be a railway line.' I said, and looked over my shoulder, just in time to see a flicker of concern in her wee sparkly eyes. 'Don't worry, you don't get trains here any more.' She smiled, reassured. 'Except the odd ghost train maybe.' I added.

'Daddy!'

'Well, hardly ever, and it's probably just a story!'

'Daddy. Stop it!'

I looked again, she had her melodramatic scared look on; she knew it was a joke and wanted me to carry on.

'Whoo whooo! Did you here that? There's a train coming. Quick, faster! Pedal faster!'

'Daddy! I can hear it. Hurry. It's coming.' We both pedalled as hard as we could, round the corner and under an old rail bridge near Johnstone. Every square inch was covered in romantic, obscene and sectarian graffiti; but most were just attempts at immortality:

Jude Woz Here.

Kevo Woz Here.

Janice and Billy Woz Here.

'Me an Daddy Woz Here!'

'Yeh! You and me, darlin. We Woz Here!'

We stopped just outside Brookfield and sat down on the grass verge for some blackcurrant and apple juice. And there it was, that solid cartoon yellow rape field, with its implausibly green tree right in the middle, and a clear blue cloudless sky above.

'When I was a wee boy, my daddy used to drive past that field and I always wanted to take a photo. Can I take one now?'

'OK. It's really pretty. It's like a painting.' I took one of just the field on its own, and one of my daughter in front.

'Just look natural.'

'OK.'

And immediately she crossed her eyes, stretched her mouth into a toothy gargoyle grin and stood on one leg. Just like I would have done aged six.

There are hardly any photographs of my dad and me for the same reason there are hardly any of me with my daughter. Cameras were boy's toys and he was the boy with the camera; Voigtlander rangefinder that only he could really use. And in the few photos that my mum took, he's all frowns and gesticulating hands, clearly issuing instructions.

'Have you got the lens cap off?' 'Make sure our heads are in!'

Bridge of Weir station hadn't been open since the 'Beeching Axe' felled it in the early 1970s. Or maybe even earlier? It was hard to roll past the old station and not get pulled into the past.

'Daddy.'

And anyway, that was the point.

'Daddy! I'm hungry.'

She dragged me back into the present.

'Hungry? Right, well, they make the best bridies in the world here.'

And so they did, at the bakery where my mum worked for a short time. Auntie Jessie, my mum's sister, was standing outside and recognized me at once.

'So this is Flora?'

'This is your great-auntie Jessie, Flora.'

'That's enough of the "great".' She took a pound coin from her purse and gave it to Flora.

'That's for you, pet, to buy what you want, and don't let your dad tell you what to spend it on.' Auntie Jessie looked at Flora, then at me. 'Well, she certainly looks like you, specially round the eyes.' It's daft I know, but a warm wave of I don't know what, swept through me, just at that recognition of me in her, her in me.

We walked the bikes up the glen to the place by the burn where I'd come so often as a child to drink watery squash with my cousins, surrounded by bare-footed aunties in cotton print dresses and shirt-sleeved uncles, their hands in their pockets. There are picnic tables now but we still sat on the grass and ate our bridies, like we used to do. And for the next hour and a half my daughter and I did everything, 'like we used to do'. We rolled down the hill like we used to do. We paddled in the burn like we used to do. She lost a shoe like I used to do. We had a stick sword fight like we used to. We played hide and seek like we used to do.

We cycled down the hill to my old house and we sat on the step, the same step that my brother and I sat on to have our picture taken in 1965; and I took a picture of my daughter and me with the camera's 10-second delay. I just made it in time and it nearly cut off the top of my head. We wandered up the road a little to my primary school, where I pointed out the Lady Bell with her big skirt up on the roof, and the railings where I'd got my head stuck twice in one week. As I was putting her helmet on, ready to go, and feeling full of food and memories, I bent down and kissed her on the nose. She looked beautiful.

'Are you sad, Daddy?'

'Do I look sad?'

'A wee bit.'

'No, not sad, darling. Just, I don't know really.'

'Mibbly?'

Mibbly. Her and her made-up words. Mibbly, meaning; happy and sad; neither one nor the other, and both together.

'Yeh, Mibbly. That's what I'm feeling, Mibbly.'

GRANDMA AND GRANDPA

Lesley Kay

GRANDPA, RESPLENDENT in his gold and cream Easter robes, read from the big book on the lectern. His straight white hair parted definitely from right to left, and his blue eyes gazed beyond the congregation, heavenwards.

'And the Lord said...'

He began again.

'And the Lord said...'

Down in the pews, Grandma nudged us. 'He's lost his place again,' she whispered, and snapped open her bag, releasing the warm brown fug of fags and polo mints. My sister and I glanced inside.

Great. Today she had Fruit Pastels.

SOMETHING IN THE AIR

Caroline Mackay

IT WAS SEPTEMBER 1988 and heading towards an Indian summer. I was a stranger in this white-washed, clay-walled public house and struck by the unfamiliarity of my surroundings.

My friend, Charlotte, had recently moved ten miles out of town to this quaint little village on Scotland's east coast. She was making a real effort to acquaint herself with the local community and had organised a fundraising disco for the playgroup. Keen for a girlie night out, I'd taken up her invitation to join her for the evening and had caught the bus through, leaving my husband, Bert, at home, in town, babysitting our two young children.

I love dancing and right at that moment it seemed like years since I had had the chance to let my hair down. The atmosphere was electric – whether due to the music, the sticky evening air, or some subliminal awareness of what was to come I'll never know, but it felt good. God, it felt good to feel free again, joyful! 'Go on!' Charlotte smiled encouragingly. 'It's too early to go home now. You don't have to, you can stay with us, you know.' Buses were few and far between in those days, and the last bus back to town was woefully early. I didn't take much persuading.

The function suite, where the disco was held, was on an upstairs floor which wasn't directly joined to the main bar. You had to leave that part of the building entirely and find your way to the downstairs public bar in order to use the phone. I pushed the door open a little hesitantly, unsure of what type of man would be propping up the counter. Even now, I regularly become tongue-tied on the receiving end of some ribald quip.

I found the phone and lifted the receiver. Of course, Bert was less than delighted to hear I wasn't coming home, but by that time I was past caring whether or not I riled him.

Truth be told, things hadn't been going well for us. Bert seemed unable to hold down a job for any length of time, putting considerable stress on our small family. In the short time we'd been together, we had managed to produce a three-year-old daughter and a six-month-old son, the latter the clichéd 'patch-over-the-cracks' baby, poor sod.

Six weeks after his birth I had found myself back at work, bringing home the bacon, when I desperately wanted to be a stay-at-home mum. I wanted a man I could rely on to back me up, not some big girl's blouse. So, what? That's no big deal, I hear you cry!

Perhaps not – and perhaps less so now in these days of house-husbands and equality for all. But back then it wasn't the way I had intended to bring up my children. It wasn't what I'd dreamed of. On my wedding day to Bert, my mother had blithely remarked, 'You don't have to go through with this, you know', and although I had since worked out that she was right – and that I shouldn't have gone through with it – I fully intended to do my best to prove her wrong. Sadly, any small respect I had had for Bert had vanished with the realisation that he was worse than useless. He didn't want to work, he didn't want to mind the children; he wanted to chill out in front of the TV all day, dreaming and spending the little I earned. Feelings were running high.

I was ripe for a fall, and fall I did.

On ending my call, I replaced the receiver and as I did so caught the eye of the most gorgeous-looking, tall, slim man I had seen in a long, long time. He was bent over the pool table lining up the black. His dark, wavy hair curled softly at the nape of his neck and his slate grey eyes focussed intensely as he took aim. Shot! A triumphant smile lit up his face as the ball clacked soundly into the pocket. I took my aim just as intensely.

It was no surprise, then, when a short while later Sean, for that was his name, followed Charlotte and me over to the disco. Don't for a moment think it was a done deal, though! Sean was striking, popular, supremely confident, he knew it and so did every other female in the room under 60! All the same, we got chatting and I discovered that he also had two children, a boy and a girl. He had recently separated from their mother and was a less of the Jack-the-lad than he first appeared.

You know when you really, really want something so bad the essence of it settles on the tip of your tongue? When every nerve cell prickles with anticipation and you can hardly breathe for need?

It was no surprise when Sean finally followed us home.

Before the month was out, we'd moved in together. I was a harlot, a home-wrecker, a whore. Two quite messy divorces followed amidst much wailing and gnashing of teeth. But it's true what they say, when you're young and in love you're indestructible.

Twenty years later, Sean and I are still together. We have a son of our own, who's now 18. We still live in the village where I met him and all five of our children remain close. We're even the proud grandparents of three-year-old baby Sean with a second grandchild due in December.

And if I hadn't gone to make that call...?

FALSIE

Ann MacLaren

IN 1958, WHEN I was six years old my parents took my grandmother, my sister, my brother and myself to Port Seton for our first holiday at the seaside. They had rented what would nowadays be called a chalet for two weeks: actually it was just a hut. It had only one room, although part of that had been sectioned off to hold a built-in double bed, and there was a cupboard with a single bed inside, where Granny would sleep; everything else was crammed into the living area, including stove, sink, table, chairs and bed-settee. The toilet was at the end of a grassy lane and was shared by all the other huts in the field. We thought it was heaven.

On our first night the three of us sat up in bed, Peter and I at the top, Margaret at the bottom, waiting for Granny to get ready for bed because she had promised she would come in beside us and tell us a story. She had a great fund of stories, my granny, none of which were of little bunnies or fairies or good little boys and girls. She favoured the ghost story, the more horrific the better, and whenever we spent the night with her she would come into bed with us and scare the wits out of us with her tales.

She climbed in beside us and as I snuggled into her I felt that something was wrong, that things weren't as they should be. Her chest felt hard against my cheek. I sat up and stared at her, noticed the flatness of her chest beside me, the roundness beside my brother. It was clear she only had one breast.

'Granny!' I was horrified. 'You've only got one of them!' At that age I probably didn't know what they were called. 'What happened to it?' Granny's eyes narrowed to give us one at a time that special stare she kept for the scariest part of her stories, and in a deep, gruff voice announced: 'It got blown off in the war.'

In the stunned silence that followed I had a clear vision of a bomb slicing past Granny's chest, hitting her breast and knocking it clean off, without a scrape or scratch to the rest of her body.

'That can't be true.' Margaret, who was ten and knew everything, was indignant. 'The war was a long time ago. And you had two of them this morning.' Granny smiled, stretched across to the chair beside the bed, and from under her clothes extracted a small flesh-coloured object that looked a bit like one of those bean bags we played with in the gym at school, only rounder and heavier. She laid this on the flat side of her chest then hoisted up her other breast to make a matching pair.

'This goes inside my brassiere,' she said. 'So nobody notices that one's missing. It's called a falsie.' Then she lifted it off her chest and threw it to Margaret at the bottom of the bed, who caught it easily and tossed it back up to Peter, who dropped it as if he thought it would bite him. Granny picked it up and passed it over to me. It felt warm and soft and a bit squishy.

I laid the falsie back on Granny's flat chest and, using my cheek to hold it in place, cuddled into her. Granny lowered her voice again and began her ghost story. I don't remember that story now. It might have been the one about the young man whose brow was sliced off and used for bacon, or the one about the old woman who dug up graves and used the bones for soup. But whatever it was, I'm sure it couldn't have been half as exciting as my first sight of Granny's falsie.

FINDING A FAMILY

Beverley Mathias

ONE BRIGHT MAY MORNING over 20 years ago, I set out to find evidence of my ancestors. The Isle of Lewis was bleak and beautiful, the road long, winding and narrow as I drove my hired car out of Stornoway and across the island, carefully watching out for, and observing, the passing places marked alongside the road. I had waited 35 years for this day, and now hoped I could find evidence of my family's life on this island. Passing flocks of black-faced sheep, slowing down for them as they crossed the road, marvelling at the wonderful views of the sea and the moors, I realised how much my great-grandfather must have missed his homeland. Eventually I reached the west side of the island, and Carloway, the village after which my great-grandfather had named his house in Australia. One street sweeping down the hill and over the water, then up the other side. Some houses either side, a road off to the right, and one to the left but no sign of a cemetery. Just back from the corner, behind the war memorial was a large Free Church, and beside it, facing the main road, was a school. It was the school in a photograph my mother had shown me of the opening of the Pentland Road. Nothing much had changed in the 80 years since then. Opposite the Free Church was a man mending a gate post. I parked the car and walked across.

'Excuse me, can you please tell me where I will find the cemetery?' was my hesitant request. The man looked at me from under his cap, carefully laid the hammer on the ground beside him, leaned on the post and spoke, 'You will be Alick Mackenzie's granddaughter and you will be looking for Ranald's grave,' he said in a soft Gaelic voice. I was stunned into silence for a few moments. How did he know who I was? Was it my Australian accent? Surely not, after all there must have been plenty of Antipodeans looking for their ancestors.

'I'm Alick's great-granddaughter but who is Ranald?' I replied.

'Come in and I will tell you about your family,' was his response.

I followed him into a sturdy two-storey stone house. The kitchen was large, warmed by a solid fuel cooker, furnished with a sofa and chairs alongside the table and cupboards one would expect. The man and his wife welcomed me, bade me sit and put in front of me crowdie, scones, biscuits, cakes – all homemade, plus a cup of strong tea.

They explained that the cemetery was on the coast about a mile or so from the village, and that Ranald was an ancestor who had been the schoolmaster in the village about 100 years before. These strangers told me of cousins I had living in Berkshire in England, of cousins in Canada, and of two elderly relatives living in sheltered accommodation in Stornoway. I was overwhelmed. When I left Stornoway the most I was expecting was one or two graves that I could use to reconstruct some of the limited family history that was in my head, and probably distorted over time. After numerous cups of tea, scones, cakes and further conversation, my head full of information only partly understood, I left to take up the story in three dimensions by visiting the cemetery and the nursing homes.

My journey took on a different aspect. I was travelling not just to see gravestones, but to meet real people, people who might remember my great-grandfather or his siblings.

The finger post on the main road simply gave the name of the area. The cemetery sits on a cliff top overlooking a spectacular beach and the Atlantic Ocean. After some investigation I found Ranald's grave and discovered that he was a Macdonald. I hadn't known I was related to the Macdonalds. But Mackenzie graves? There were plenty, but nobody related to me.

Driving across the island again I thought about which of the nursing homes to visit. I had verbal instructions as to how to find each of them, but knew there was insufficient time in the day to visit both. From something that had been said during that incredible conversation in the kitchen at Carloway, I decided to visit Dun Berisay to find out about one of these previously unknown relatives. On enquiring at reception I was told I could visit Mrs Macleod of Tarbert (there are so many Macleods, Mackenzies, Smiths, Morrisons, that they are identified by their place of birth or residence). I was taken down a corridor to her room and told she was bedridden but quite alert. After knocking gently on the door, the nurse went in and said there was a visitor.

'You're Grace's girl,' said the elderly lady in the bed. 'Yes I am,' I replied, stunned again at what others seemed to know about me. It could not have been my Australian accent this time, as I had not even opened my mouth.

We talked for ages, until she was too tired to talk any more. I found out that my grandmother and other Mackenzie relatives in Australia had kept in touch with these relatives in Stornoway and Reading and that they knew of me, and my two brothers. I knew nothing of them. I found out that the great-great aunt who had sent me my fifth birthday present lived in 'the granite house' in Cromwell Street in Stornoway. And I discovered that some of my Mackenzie relatives were buried in the cemetery just outside the town.

Returning to the place where I was staying I mulled over what I had learnt that day about the family I did not know existed. I had gone to find gravestones, but I had returned knowing about living relatives. I will never forget the sentence spoken to me that morning.

'Come away in and I will tell you about your family.'

Moran taing Iain.

THINGS WE CAN BE SURE ARE OF
NO IMPORTANCE

Katy McAulay

I AM 26 and I have bought my first home; a one bed flat just big enough for two.

We are new to this. Bed, bookcase, bits and bobs cobbled together from previous residencies we rented solo make do for the most part and we are just fine.

The living room is lacking. Just an old television, a fireplace we attach fairy lights to, and one sofa. It's really an armchair. Blue once, it can become a credible bed for one when its innards are wrestled with, but in sofa mode: too small. He is six-two. In bed, arms, legs and heads cradle in the appropriate places and his heartbeat sings me to sleep. On this sofa elbows and knees surface. Necks are cricked as a new geometry is sought.

The responsibility of this purchase is more squarely mine than his. I feel it. Though we do not refer to it in these terms, it is my money and it is my flat, and yet home for the both of us. When he can, he'll put in for half of it, or we'll buy another together, but for now, that's the way it's worked out, and we are just fine.

We work different schedules. One day in our allocation of Christmas holidays has to be earmarked for the purpose. I hire a car to make the sweep around DFS speedier.

Before we leave we measure up. We snake the tape around doorways – living room and front – making sure we can accommodate our new arrival and we decide from the brochure that the cheapest one will be just fine.

It's a drizzly Saturday – one of the depressed days between Christmas and New Year. On the shop front a plastic banner screams BETTER THAN HALF-PRICE SALE! We are there for opening time; he wants to go tenpin bowling in the afternoon.

There is free champagne at the door. Salesmen ooze out of every crevice. We breeze past offers of help, seeking out the deal we have planned to buy into.

It's girly. The aubergine colour from the picture is more pink in real life. It's freakishly narrow too, like a church pew, or pigeon perch. We circulate. The second cheapest option is only available in light grey. It looks like office furniture. The floor is becoming crowded. A glass of bubbly might make this easier, but I'm driving.

We drift. He is distracted by a huge leather thing that could swallow me up, and then we consider a red one for a while. It's double the price of the chair we came for, but it's comfortable at least. The salesmen sniff victory.

We get to the filling in forms stage and I can't do it. The numbers aren't making sense. What happens if it won't fit in the front door? We've got a very narrow front door, I remind him. We've been in here three hours, he tells me.

I need more time. A tape measure. Some guts.

'Should we try Ikea?'

His face falls but he trails obediently across the dripping car park and folds himself into the Kia Picante we have rented. I catch sight of myself in the mirror. Embarrassment is swimming in my eyes.

At Ikea the options crowd in. Measurements, prices, colours, opportunity cost. This one is £75 more but the covers are washable. There are no windows in this place but I can sense the dusk gathering outside, waiting to rush at us. Do we have time to nip back to DFS? Look at the red one again – make sure? We trudge to our vehicle again, a metre's worth of air between us. His cheeks are red from the cold. I want to rest my face against them, cool my own burning cheeks with his, but I don't.

Inside the doorway of DFS I consider a new option. Was this one here earlier? I don't remember it. He chooses a recliner and tips himself back, showing me the soles of his boots. The champagne has run out. We are both weak with hunger. It will cost an extra £114 to have the red one sprayed with some stuff to stop it staining if we spill. When we spill.

We consider the pink one again. He scuffs his boot against the floor and says quietly, we won't make it to bowling then?

I'm out in the dark car park and scrabbling the key in the lock and I heave the seatbelt across me and turn the headlights on and I would drive the thing into the back of the McDonald's ahead of me if only it wasn't a hire car so instead I switch the engine off and open my mouth and begin to scream. He stares at me in astonishment as I yell and yell, unable to hold it in because I don't want to spend time in which I am not working looking at sofas and I don't want to care whether something will match with my curtains and I didn't think something so ridiculous could be so difficult and I don't understand when I stopped being a teenager.

When I am finished we are both quiet. It's pouring; the windscreen and window on my side opaque with steam. I can't look at him. In the tiny space we inhabit, he is miles away.

And so I turn the key and the engine starts again and I switch the demister on and swipe my sleeve across the windscreen and then I manoeuvre us carefully away.

On the motorway back to Glasgow he turns on the radio and inserts one of his Tom Waits tapes into the deck.

'I will love you forever,' Tom sings. He winds down the window and turfs the DFS brochure out into the rainy dark and then he reaches over and gently unpeels one of my hands from the wheel.

SIX AND A HALF POUNDS

Joanne Ross

DAYS ARE LONG and hot. I'm still a teenager, almost ages with Lady Diana Spencer who is to marry Prince Charles in July. Luckily for me big hair, baggy dungarees and loose fitting sailor dresses are all in fashion. It is Thursday 28 May 1981.

I wake and I'm bleeding. I tell my mother. Oh, she says, that's what you call a show of blood; you must be going into labour. She insists on driving me to the hospital where the doctor says, you first time mothers are always having false labours. A quick examination and he tells me I'm not due for another two months. But I tell him I've worked out the dates. Nonsense, says he, I'm far too small, he has the scan report and I'll be lucky to have the baby next month, never mind next week. He packs me off with a plastic container in which I'm to collect urine samples and return in a fortnight. 'Bloody typical,' my mother says.

We're hardly back in the door when the pain starts. It could be contractions my mother says and goes to phone my auntie Mary just to make sure. She tells my auntie Mary she thinks I am having contractions. Apparently contractions are something quite exciting. By the time my auntie Mary arrives I'm having contractions every 15 minutes. If she's having contractions, my auntie Mary says, I'm a monkey's uncle. 'Bloody typical,' my mother says.

When the contractions that maybe aren't contractions at all start coming every ten minutes, my mother phones the hospital and the father-to-be. 'Bring her in,' the hospital said. My auntie Mary has terrified the life out of me with all her talk of the contractions that should have me doubled over with pain, I don't want to go. 'If you're having me on,' my mother says.

First, the doctor examines me internally, in the middle of one of the contractions that maybe isn't a contraction at all. I scream so loud they probably heard me in the waiting room. The doctor tells me to be quiet. It is not that painful. Bloody typical my mother would have said.

Next I have to be prepared, ie., ablutions and change into a stupid-looking long white bib with sleeves before I'm reunited with the father-to-be. We're put in the waiting room with other expectant parents and I'm still not sure if I'm really having the contractions. The nurse comes round with a menu card. I tick for soup, roast beef and ice cream. When I hand the card back, she says, 'Oh, you're only allowed ice cream, you can't eat when you're in the advanced stages of labour.' Advanced stages of labour, is it? I don't know anything about the advanced stages of labour and don't like to ask. Must be the contractions.

Before I know it, no ice cream or anything, we're being marched along to the delivery room. They strap me up to a monitor and make sure I'm as uncomfortable as possible. The midwife snaps, 'Why didn't you tell us your waters had broken?' Eh! I had just been for a very long pee but I didn't know anything about broken waters. Apparently I'm dilated and the head's engaged. Dilated. That's a new one. I don't know anything about heads being engaged either. The midwife wants to know what on earth do they teach at the antenatal classes these days? Antenatal class versus Elvis Costello live at the Apollo. No contest. I always had far more important things to worry about. The midwife tsk tsks and leaves us alone in the delivery room. The father-to-be is taking advantage of the gas and air. 'That's no bad,' he giggles.

Suddenly the contractions my auntie Mary was talking about happen and I think I'm dying a horrible death. I scream. The midwife comes running in. She tries to drown me out. There's a woman next door who has been in labour for 17 hours, you've only been here half an hour. I don't care. I'm out of control. She slaps me on the leg, tells me to calm down and tries to suffocate me with the gas and air. It doesn't help. I feel like I want to go to the toilet but she won't let me. It's the baby coming. She tells me not to push. I try to escape the pain by humming a tune, humming louder and louder, the words boiling in my head, stand and deliver, your baby or your life.

I hate Adam and the Ants. The father-to-be wants to know where's the doctor? Three nurses appear but no doctor. The midwife says, 'push' and 'don't push', 'push'. 'Aaah, aaah,' I moan and groan with the pain. I push and push until a wee bloody head squeezes out. Just another push, another push and next thing I know a wee bloody bairn is screaming for its life and they're strapping my legs up in holsters so they can stitch me up. At last the doctor arrives. It's like a butcher's shop. There's blood dripping off the table on to the floor. In my whole life I've never seen so much blood. Didn't know I had so much blood. I pass out. They bring me round. They offer me tea and toast while they're mopping up the blood.

I wake up in the maternity ward. No baby. I panic and ring the bell. The nurse says something about incubators and premature births. They put a rubber ring on a wheelchair and wheel me down to see. It's a miracle. She has thick black hair like mine on her tiny little head and teeny wee hands and feet, long eyelashes and deep blue eyes. Just perfect. At visiting time my mother makes a big fuss about haemorrhages and how at six and a half pounds my baby is not premature. It turns out she's right. 'Bloody typical,' my mother says.

MERMAIDS

Tasca Shadix

NOTHING PARTICULARLY unusual happened on 17 August 2007. My husband went to work early, leaving me alone with our then almost-three-year-old daughter, Bo, who spent most of the morning wearing only a pair of baggy pants and a tutu into which she had tucked, for reasons known only to her, a toy duck and a dishtowel.

We played with Play-Doh that day. We read stories. We watched television and ate a good snack, followed by a decadent lunch of tomatoes, carrots, fresh bread from the local bakery, a deliciously creamy avocado, cheese, and (in my case) an entire tin of sardines. Then we made a huge smoothie, the consistency of sorbet, and ate every last bit of it. If either of us so much as licked another item of food, I imagine we would have exploded.

We took a bath together, or rather, she joined me as I bathed and read a news magazine. I set it aside, and we had a great time discussing mermaids: 'Can they walk, really?' And 'How do they wash their hair?' We pondered the question 'Who is young and who is old?' and also her favourite philosophical topic, Death, also known as Going into the Ground. Everyone goes into the ground 'she knows that much' but she has many questions about the topic. 'When was there not any people? I wasn't there. I want to know,' she asked me. And 'Who will be there when all the people are dead?'

I don't remember what I told her. I hope it was the truth, that I have no idea. But if I stammered out some fumbling speculation about the universe, I hope she won't hold me to it.

After our bath, as we sat at her little crafts table, I was playing the latest Be Good Tanyas CD, and pointing out to Bo the instruments we could hear in the songs. I told her that this was my favourite music, and that it made me want to dance in my chair.

She started swaying in her own chair. 'It makes me do it, too,' she said, and we sat there for a lovely moment, dancing in our chairs.

'It also makes me do this.' I closed my eyes and bobbed my head.

She nodded solemnly. 'It kind of makes your head dance.'

That statement made me so proud. I thought, she already has the poet's gift for concise truth! Well, really it's probably just that poets have retained the knack of observing the world as children do. But...yes, Bo, it does kind of make your head dance, doesn't it?

Sometimes I feel inadequate because I'm not an extremely skilful person, and I wonder what tools for life I will be able to pass on to my daughter. I'm a disinterested cook, a tech illiterate, I can't play music or fix cars or sew or garden or build things with wood. I can speak French and execute a mean karate kick, but I'm hardly a role model for choosing practical, level-headed pursuits to enhance one's life for skill and profit.

However, on that day, I could sense it, could almost put my finger on what I'm teaching Bo about life. Or rather, we taught each other, that day, about food, and music, and beauty, and whimsy, and long, quiet mornings with plenty of time to think. Surely those, too, are valuable things to share.

It was just another day with my daughter, no more representative of our time together than the days when I'm crabby and hurried, or she's whingey and contrary, but what a sweet day it was. Write it down, I told myself. Don't forget to write it down. You'll remember it as one of the best days of your life.

OH! CHRISTMAS TREE...
OH! CHRISTMAS TREE

Mae Stewart

IT WAS 1950. I'd been living in Fintry housing scheme in Dundee, with my family, for about a year, and our first Christmas in the 'new hoose' was approaching.

My mother decided she would push the boat out, and we were all to set off for the Arcade in town to get a really good Christmas tree, now we had the room.

'We' being my wee brother Johnnie (six), my wee sister Carol (in the tansad), and me (ten). And leading the group, of course, the lady of the house.

We duly got off the bus at Shore Terrace, and crossed the road to look at the trees that sat outside the door of the Arcade.

Well there were big trees, wee trees, skinny trees and fat trees.

Then she spots it. Nudges me. 'Will yeh tak a look at that tree, now that's a real dinger!'

The 'real dinger' was just that. It was really really green. It had a huge trunk. It was enormous. We fell in love with it.

'How much tae tak it aff yehr hands?' says she to the Arcade man, preparing for battle.

'Och! Well,' says he. 'It's the same price as a' the rest, but yeh'll hae tae move it now, fir Eh canna store it fir yeh.'

'Done,' says my mother as we nabbed the bargain of the year. She turns to my brother and me.

'Tak meh bag, an ain o yeh haud the tansad, till Eh get this tree manoeuvred across it.' And in a couple of minutes my wee sister vanished under a pine forest, with just room for her to peek out on the world. My mother gives us directions. 'Ain o' yeh get the tap, an ain o' yeh get the bottom, tae balance it, till weh get tae the bus stop. Are yeh haudin on? Right aff weh go! Wagons Ho!'

We arrived at the bus stop. And encountered our first hurdle. The bus conductor.

'Geezo, Mrs, thir's nae weh that thing's comin on the bus.'

'Says WHA?'

'The sehze o' the bus says, that's wah! Fir Eh'll no get it in the cubbie.'

And he was right. Try as he might. It would not go in the 'cubbie'.

'Right,' says my mother to us. 'Then weh'll jist hae tae get the tram car an walk fae Maryfield.'

By this time it was getting dark, and I was beginning to go off this tree big time, and we were all getting weary, but mission 'get-the-tree-hame' had to be accomplished. We were speaking my mother here.

Anyway, we got this giant of a thing on the tramcar right enough. The tram conductor had to fold down two rows of seats muttering away to us, 'Guid joab it's no the busy time'. He just got ignored.

Fifteen minutes later when we got to the terminus at the top of the Forfar Road, it had started to pour down that damp feechie sleet.

'Nearly hame now,' says mother, convincing none of the troops.

My wee brother walked on uncomplaining but getting very downcast. I got thumped for mumping about my gloves getting soaked, and me having cold fingers, and got instructed; 'Bla on them, we'll be hame afor yeh kin say Jeck Roabson.' I was too tired to care about any Jeck Roabson, whoever he was, as we trudged on.

The only happy one was my sister. She was wrapped up like a wee bird, nesting in the tree. And look like a bird she did with all the pine cones sticking to her pink, fluffy angora bonnet and matching mitts.

Finally – we arrived home, and my father must've been looking out for us because he was at the door when we got there.

'Whit the hell's that? Sherwood Forest?'

'Whit the hell diz it look like? An niver mind a' that, jist help iz get it in the hoose.'

'An, Mary, how dae yeh suggest Eh get a 12 tae 14 fuht tree intae a hoose that's only 10 fuht fae the flair tae the ceilin?'

She stopped dead. I stopped dead. My wee brother burst into tears. My sister, the wee pink bird, was oblivious, lucky her.

We'd humphed that tree for what seemed the same distance as it took Hannibal to get his elephants over the Alps. And it was too big!

So we small group of pioneers stood looking out the living room window as my father sawed off the extra feet and re-pinned the bottom of the tree to its crossed wooden slats, then dragged it through the door and stood it up in the living room.

'Och now, admit it, diz that no look jist great!' enthuses my mother, beaming at all and sundry, including the tree. 'Nae herm done. It widda been worse if it hid been too wee.'

I can still picture my father, as he passed by my brother and me, looking at us, then laughing, as he walked into the kitchen to put away his hammer and saw.

BURN DOWN THE DISCO

Allan Wilson

IT LIT UP THE Glasgow skyline as the last bars of the music played and hundreds of us watched in empathy as this pillar of our youth faded. A lot was lost that night, much more than just the building and the dancefloors and the booze, but romances in blossom and nervous first kisses. The scent of perfume on collars, hot breath on lips. Jealous glances, girls and boys and boys and girls.

I watched you on the dancefloor with a boy. I wanted to be his hands as they slid up and down your petite waist. I longed to be his neck as your warm breath caressed it. Most of all I wanted to be his eyes.

You danced so close and then you danced apart. You moved like an angel with a devil's smile. I could only imagine the rasp of your laugh and the touch of your tender thigh as you danced to the beat, the beat, the beat of my heart. God, it pounded. I was on the balcony overlooking the entire dancefloor and I stood, faux cool, with my friend Craig. We drained 60 pence vodka mixes and watched.

'Mate...mate...there's one. Schwing!' He lusted at girl after girl. He poked me, I tried to stay focussed. I wanted you to feel the spark and then, then you looked up and for a second I felt my hands on your waist, your breath teasing my neck, your eyes choosing me and that was it.

You coyly looked away, but then you looked back up and smiled and I laughed cause you'd caught me staring so I hoped you would laugh when I put my hand over my eyes all embarrassed. When I moved it you were still watching me and you were smiling as well. You kept dancing as you watched me, your expression changing from laughter to smirking to coy to sexy. A drill couldn't have broken my grin when you waved for me to come down.

And then the lights went up and I thought 3.00 a.m. had skipped the queue. I turned to the dancefloor again to look for you but there was some sort of melee and people on the dancefloor weren't dancing but were running aimlessly. It was as if they'd been born for the dark.

And then it started to rain. The vodka was dancing through, serenading my bloodstream and I didn't know what was what. I remember hearing boys screaming 'fire' and girls opening umbrellas to stop the sprinkler water from curling their hair.

'Mate, it's all gone tits up. We're getting out, they're evacuating.' I went with Craig and got caught in the current of bodies squeezing and squirming their way down the stairs. I remember looking but I couldn't see you. There were bodies heaving over bodies and the screams in my ear made me start to realise that something serious was happening.

I was caught in the heaving crowd that huddled together at the joint between Sauchiehall and Pitt Street. I looked as far as I could but you weren't there. The wind was swirling and the smoke pirouetted down the street bringing the scent of burning night with it. The police moved us all back from the mouth of the scene and we could no longer see the shack, only hear the snap, crackle and last bars of pop. There was a lot of chatter from the crowd, lots of screams and whoops. There was talk of people trapped inside the building and I began to panic thinking it could have been you. I tortured myself with a hundred what ifs. What if I'd come down to speak to you? What if I'd had the courage to say hi? What if I hadn't had so much to drink? What if you were ash, blowing in the wind?

And then, shivering in a doorway: you. You had a white coat on, thick, like sheepskin. In one of your hands you carried a portfolio case and the boy you were with, he carried one too. In his other hand was another hand. Not a pretty, dainty hand like yours, but a hairy hand. A man's hand!

It seemed natural, to go and ask if you were alright. It was only when I got within ten feet or so of you, only when you looked straight at me that I realised how weird me talking to you as if I knew you would make me appear. I nearly spun on my heel and turned back into the crowd but I'd lost you once and was loathe to do it again. I took a deep breath. Shuffling my feet, looking away, I approached. You just kept smiling. Your smile so pretty. And it was weird cos we just talked as if the boys weren't there and I said Hi and you just laughed a little and said Hiya back. I muttered something about wanting to buy you a drink and you poked my ribs saying it was a bit late now. With each word we got closer. There were sirens wailing in the background and the crowds were swelling and yelping so I moved in to hear you and I felt your breath on my neck. You said something and I missed it so I came in really close, my hand falling inside your jacket, brushing against your waist. I still don't know who moved in first, and you'll say me though I'm not so sure, but somehow our faces were touching and you laughed, recoiling when my cold nose leant against yours but then you stopped laughing and looked straight at me. And I kissed you. And that was it.

As a fallen pillar of our youth lit up the sky like a thousand shooting stars and our generation surged just feet from us, trotting away one by one, there were two people oblivious to it all, safe in the warmth of each other's arms, sharing their first kiss.

Society

DEALING WITH THE CHANGE

(anonymous)

FOR THE NEXT COUPLE of days I would be working down south. I set out around noon to drive from Edinburgh to the Black Country, a journey of four and a half to five hours. After passing Penrith, I left the M6 and drove on the A6 instead until, shortly after three o'clock, I pulled into the car park of a rural pub, and taking my grip with me, went inside.

I ordered a soft drink and a sandwich, and sat down on a bar stool to read *The Scotsman*. When the sandwich came I ate half of it immediately.

Leaving my food and drink on the bar, and the paper on my stool, I picked up the grip and went to the gents, where I entered a cubicle and locked the door behind me. Quickly removing my socks and shoes, trousers and shirt, I was left standing there wearing only the black lace panties I had selected that morning.

From the grip I took out my change. First was an eight strap suspender belt, which after I had hooked it up, had to be adjusted to be under the panties. Only then I was able to attach the barely black stockings. Next I slipped on a matching black lace bra (matching the panties not the belt) followed by my three-inch kitten heel sandals.

Now I have been dressing for years and still nothing beats the sensation of standing up in high heels and the effect they have on my posture. I always feel so slinky and sexy when I put on my heels. In reality, I know I'm a 16 stone middle-aged bald rugby player, who at that moment looks totally ridiculous, but that thought is never allowed to spoil my special moment.

I donned a powder blue strappy top and dark blue miniskirt and finished off by loading my bra with homemade falsies.

While I folded my male clothes neatly in the grip I heard the door to the loo open. A visitor used the facilities, washed and then left again.

I smoothed myself down and, unlocking the cubical door, stepped out into the general toilet area. Standing before the mirror, I quickly applied some bright red lipstick (similar to the colour I had used on my toenails earlier that morning) and attached a pair of 'Pat Butcher' clip-on earrings. Both were deliberately selected to look trashy and cheap. Now I was ready for that delicious and slightly dangerous moment.

When I'm dressing in public, I always try to select safe locations. Places like this, a remote pub in the middle of the afternoon where the chances are that the clientele will be middle-aged or older couples. I try to avoid groups of youths or rough men and out of a sense of fairness, young families. I don't think I would have liked the 'Daddy, why is that man wearing a dress?' question.

But no matter how careful I am in selecting a location, no matter how benign it was when I went to the loo, there is always some apprehension in that moment before I step out.

I opened the door and stepped back into the bar. A quick scan revealed that there were no newcomers. A middle-aged couple of barflies chatting to the barmaid, and two old coffin dodgers, sitting on opposite sides of the barroom, nursing pints to avoid having to go back home.

My heels clicked on the floor as I walked back to my stool at the bar. As I crossed the room I was aware of the barmaid making frantic gestures to the couple to turn round and look at me. One of the coffin dodgers stared at me without displaying any interest at all.

The barmaid gave me her 'winning' smile and the man of the couple turned round to look at me. I hoisted myself back onto the stool taking care to keep my knees pressed together. I wouldn't want to look silly.

'Fancy dress is it?'

'No' I told the twonk. 'I just like wearing a frock'. I fiddled with my bra strap which was twisted and once straightened, let it snap back against my shoulder.

'Very nice too,' responded his dimwitted companion. When I first encountered banal comments like this I would get irritated, but then I realised that they were simply masking their own embarrassment. Now, I just try to field the comments but on occasion, if the individual seems particularly inept, I camp it up and try to increase their discomfort.

'Oh do you really like it?' I asked, addressing myself to her. I slipped off the stool and provocatively smoothed my clothes, from just below my bust and right down over my skirt, never taking my eyes off her.

She blustered and the barmaid tried to come to her rescue. 'I like your tights,' she said, desperately trying to pretend that this was a normal conversation.

'Gotcha!' I thought. Suppressing a wicked smile, I lifted up my right foot and rested it firmly on the top spar of the bar stool next to the couple.

'Do you like them?' I asked. 'I haven't shaved my legs for a while. Does that spoil the look?' I said to her.

She was speechless. Meanwhile, Twonk was verifying that what I was wearing was not in fact tights, but stockings secured by an array of garter straps.

I tired of the game and returned to my own stool to finish my sandwich and drink, and received no further cretinous comments.

The rest of the journey was undertaken in female dress, and was entirely uneventful. When I arrived at my hotel, one of these lodge type places, I knew I was about to experience another first. Tonight would be the first time I had actually arrived at a hotel en-femme and gone through the whole check-in thing, dressed. The car park indicated the hotel was pretty busy.

I took a deep breath and stepped out of the car.

FREE AT LAST

Sheila Adamson

I WENT TO THE opening of the Scottish Parliament today. 9 October 2004, a wee moment of history. It was the first time I'd seen the building properly, even though they've been building it round the corner from me for the last however many years. Now the hoardings and cranes and cement mixers have been cleared away and in their place we suddenly have ponds, grass and this big, weird collection of architecture. It's certainly different. Not sure if I like it yet. Not sure at all.

I read what the architect's widow said about it and sometimes I feel I know what she's getting at and sometimes I feel she's on a different planet. She said the building was trying to disguise the fact that it had to have walls. As if walls were a bad thing for a building to have. She said it wasn't a rigid hierarchical structure but looser, like boats in a harbour. Doesn't she think that Scottish politics is quite disorganised enough? She said she and her husband wanted to give the Scottish people something that lives up to the hundreds of years we've had to wait. To me the building feels very un-Scottish. That may prove to be no bad thing; maybe we need to change.

There's a lot of optimism on a day like today, which is also not natural for Scotland. Let's face it, what are we famous for? We're dour. We're dogged. We revel in dry humour and taking the piss out of our friends. We don't get carried away. If Jesus appeared in the second coming and offered us the kingdom of heaven we'd say, 'Aye, but will it work? How much will it cost?'

It cost £430 million. Apparently that's about £85 a head. When I heard this I was surprised. If someone had come to me ten years ago and said I could have a Scottish Parliament for £85 I'd have called it a bargain. Yes, it would have been even more of a bargain if they hadn't made such a pig's ear of the construction, but it still feels worth it to me. I couldn't go back to the old days of Westminster rule.

Others obviously could. There were protesters in the crowd at Horse Wynd with placards complaining about the cost. The police seemed keen to move them away, perhaps out of sight of the TV cameras. That leaves a bad taste, what is a parliament about if it isn't democracy? What worries me more is the quiet but pernicious niggling from the sidelines. There was a man next to me who spent the entire time swapping cynical comments with his son and slagging off people in the procession. They thought they were being clever. I wanted to enjoy the day, I did enjoy the day, more than I expected. They wanted to criticise it. I nearly turned to them and berated them. I nearly said to the boy, 'Don't you know this is the best country in the world to live in? Can't you be glad?'

Of course, that's a reckless claim to make. The best country? There are several other perfectly nice countries around the world. Nevertheless, I would rather have Scotland. It suits me. And the pre-match entertainment was firing me up, putting a tear in my eye. Three tangerine-kilted tenors belted out Scottish songs, ending with a rousing '500 Miles'. I had to laugh at their spirited rendition of 'The Deil's Awa wi the Exciseman'. Does this mean in the new Scotland there will be no tax?

Banners in the procession attempted to proclaim our national values, which naturally prompted more scorn from my carping companions. I was interested to see we believe in Compassion, Wisdom, Justice and Integrity. I can sign up to that, although I fear we'll have trouble living up to it. Especially the politicians. 'I wonder who comes up with these bland slogans?' sneered Mr Negative.

I didn't hear what he would have come up with that was better.

The procession was winding to a halt. Wheelchair users who had stoically bumped their way over the cobbles of the Royal Mile collected at the edge of the road, their path blocked by a kerb. The parliament welcomes everyone in with its inclusive architecture, but only in a metaphorical sense.

I went home to watch the ceremony itself on TV. It was good. Edwin Morgan's poem was excellent, spelling out what we don't want from the parliament. The droopy mantra, 'It wisnae me.' But more to the point is what we do want. Jack McConnell, not normally the most natural of public speakers, spoke well and emotionally. He wants us to take pride in ourselves and be positive. I imagined Mr Negative, trundling off with his son, happily complaining about everything. Maybe that's as positive as we get in Scotland.

But we have our sentimental side. For the finale to the ceremony 'Auld Lang Syne' was sung and everyone linked hands and joined in. Normally to gain that sense of heart-warming togetherness you have to be drunk on Hogmanay. My heart was thoroughly warmed today. Everybody was belting out the tune, bouncing hands and wishing well. Even the royal pursuivants or whatever they're called, and the bloke who carries the mace. The only two who stood apart were the Queen herself and the presiding officer, George Reid, next to her. I don't know if George offered a hand to his trusty fiere or if he was afraid to. Nobody touches the royal person. I felt sorry for her. Left out again.

So who knows how the parliament will get on? How many good ideas will be realised, and how many will be knocked down by the Mr Negatives? Will auld acquaintance quickly be forgotten? I feel I've seen the best and worst of my country all in one day, and I suspect I know the answer.

GOLD DUST

Kate Aimes

DAYS LIKE THESE, they're priceless. Gold dust. In Glasgow the tenements are glowing red in the dawn and the windows of my bedroom are running wet with breath. Hamish next door is an insomniac. He's been up for hours composing delicious, sad melodies that sneak under the gap in his door to entertain anyone awake to listen. He'll be asleep by noon, cradling his head on the keys. Wattie on the top floor was clearing out the basement yesterday and will wake late, feeling content in a job well done. He'll gather up his photographic equipment and drive somewhere to take pictures of ordinary things, making them extraordinary in that way he does. In number 70, Catriona is picking her outfit for the day. She has such lovely shoes. Marisa lives across the road and is imagining how the first flat she will share with her husband will look. She hopes for an attic conversion with three bedrooms. Someplace cosy with a workroom for Stuart when he needs the quiet. At the bottom of the hill, number 156, Emily's hedge is freshly cut. This month's edition of *Vanity Fair* will be delivered at 11.45 a.m. Birds in full song in the Botanics and the Meadows and the woods at Tentsmuir and on the Isle of Skye where Donald is looking out of the window, listening to the kettle boil. The Polish bakery that makes the bread Feliks likes to bring on Tuesdays is opening its doors. The smell of this morning's loaves washes the Edinburgh cobblestones. Sandy's city allotment is a treasure trove of beetroot and tatties and fresh peas that ping across the kitchen when Linda tries to shell them. Dandy the pony waiting for his breakfast in Stromness. Graeme playing a game of horse with Kate, which is difficult because there aren't many horses on the streets of London town. In Los Angeles, Mike will be finishing up work and telephoning Christin to see what he can bring in for dinner. She dreams of the meringues with cream she ate in Kember and Jones in the West End of Glasgow; knows she will have to return for another visit next year!

Today is the day Ellie remembers how it felt to be able to put her head under water without holding her nose for the first time. Jude will show Ailsa the pair of earrings she treated herself to on the way home from work. Gary will discover a first edition of the *Dark Side of the Moon* he'd forgotten he had, a receipt for the purchase from the Paisley branch of Woolworths tucked inside the cover. Today is a birthday and the second day of a fortnight's break in Nerja and a new leaf and a first kiss and a month managed without cigarettes. It's the day Vicky works out that the red elastic bands she keeps finding on the pavement outside her front door are used to keep bundles of mail together and then discarded by the postman. It's when a handwritten letter is received and Agnes smells the flowers newly laid on her grave and the first time it's possible to think fondly about the man who cheated and the day the words 'The End' are written on a script. Today is all this and more; imagined and real. It could have been anything, and it still might. It's got potential, style, legs, plans, swagger – today's got ideas above its station. It's been waiting forever to happen and now it's finally here and it won't be back. What do you feel like doing?

A RARE DAY

Joyce Anderson

THE BUS WAS IDLING at the terminus when the boy clambered aboard. Most of the seats were occupied by women laden with groceries. We all had one thing in common; we were cold and damp. The boy too, was weighed down by bulging plastic bags; and he had great difficulty getting his fare from the depths of his threadbare denims.

'Dae ye go by Ibrox, pal?' he asked the driver with a wide grin.

'Aye,' he smiled in reply.

'Wan tae there then. Ta.'

The driver dropped the money into the machine, and indicated the ticket curling out. Taking it, the boy started up the aisle of the bus. He was tall and thin, aged about 18. His long, jet-black hair was plastered to his skull, courtesy of the heavy downpour. He was shivering. Silently, I sympathised with him, as I too was soaked. He walked to the back of the bus and found a seat. The quiet of shared damp misery once more settled over the passengers. Suddenly, he was up on his feet. The woman in the seat beside him glanced up in fright.

'Dae ye like melons, missus?' he asked her.

In his hand was one of the plastic bags, open to reveal a large melon cut into slices. He reached in, drew out a slice, and handed it to her.

'Thanks, son,' she beamed and tucked in with gusto.

Walking down the aisle, he handed out slice after slice until everyone had one. The driver got one too, and after several bites, started the bus. The boy stood beside him.

'Ah got a rerr bargain o' they melons at the Barras,' he told his delighted audience.

'The man sellin' them was fed up wi' the weather. He told us they were going cheap. Ah got four bags o' them fur a pound. Ah would've got mair but ah couldnae cairry ony mair.'

His young face was shining with delight as he relived his great bargain. The woman behind me called to him.

'They're just luvly, son. Am fair drooned in juice.' Slurping, she tried to stem the flow.

'Haud oan!' he called.

He raced up the bus and, in seconds, was back with the tissues the melons had been wrapped in.

'There ye are. Ye kin wipe yourself wi' them.'

'Ta son. You've thoat o' everythin'.'

He gave a nod and returned to his seat. I sat in silence, deep in thought. I found it hard to describe what I had just witnessed. It was an amazing act of kindness, but it was much more than that. There he was, undernourished and poorly dressed for the atrocious weather, but what he had, he had shared cheerfully and unselfishly with us all. He had said he had got a great bargain. What we had got was priceless.

I got off the bus at my stop and watched as it dwindled into the distance. I was soaked anew as I walked along in the heavy rain. I should have been miserable. I wasn't. Inside me was a warm joyous feeling, an all encompassing glow. It stayed with me for the rest of that day, and is now fixed permanently in that place where best memories are stored.

THE FRIENDLY BUTLER

John Breckenridge

YOU KNOW HOW IT IS; the party has finished, you've put your girl on the last bus home after a close and passionate goodnight kiss but your mind and body are buzzing. Surely someone's still partying – it's only 1.00 a.m. for God's sake!

On high alert you walk out of George Square, along St Vincent Street and into Renfield Street, heading back up to your flat. You reach into your pocket for a cigarette. Good – she hasn't smoked them all. Pulling one out of the packet you reach into your pocket for matches. Damn, damn and damn. No matches and you're dying for a smoke. You look around and there's a smartly dressed chap, smoking a cigarette and walking down the other side of the street. You cross over, and waving your unlit cigarette, you stop him and ask for a light.

He smiles, reaches into his pocket and produces a gold lighter, coaxing it into flame with a practised flick of his thumb. Cigarette lit; he speaks to you in a well modulated English accent. Not normal in Renfield Street at a quarter past one on a Sunday morning. You start talking and find a shared, passionate interest in having things to do after 1.00 a.m. on a Sunday morning.

The talking continues past that point where you say thanks for the light and go on your respective ways. He asks if you fancy going back to his place where he claims to have some amazing whiskies that are just asking to be sampled. You think it isn't a bad idea but worry about how far you have to walk. He says he'll pay for a taxi. You wonder for a moment...and then agree.

Twenty minutes later the taxi turns into the driveway of a large South-side mansion. You look at him enquiringly – he says he lives here and directs the taxi round to the back. We get out and he unlocks the door, motioning you inside with a finger to his lips. People are asleep.

He guides you through to a small sitting room furnished comfortably with battered green leather armchairs spread around a smart gas fire which he lights. You sit down and he disappears, only to return with a tray on which stand a crystal jug of water, crystal glasses, one bottle of Glenmorangie and another of The Macallan. Bliss! Students can't afford luxuries like this.

Glasses filled, the discussion resumes. You ask about the house, is it his? He laughs and says that it belongs to His Lordship, that he is His Lordship's butler and that we are in his quarters, the Butler's Pantry. As he explains further you are amazed the perks of the job. He claims the salary is quite reasonable, but that is only a start as he also lives, eats and drinks and dresses at His Lordship's expense. You ask about being a butler, what do you do, do you run His Lordship's household? He seems to find your questions funny but explains the running of the household and it seems that he is His Lordship's right hand in the house and on the estate.

You then tell him about your degree courses, the professors and lecturers, life in a student flat, your flatmates and their funny little ways, the feeling of being perennially hard up and the dodges required to survive in some sort of style. Dodges like a wasp in a matchbox that can be conveniently 'found' in your rice towards the end of your curry, the resultant protest ending with a free meal.

As the conversation develops, you are astonished at the breadth of his reading and knowledge. He then starts in on the Macmillan Government. As a debater and a member of all of the main University political clubs you enjoy this and soon you are going at it hammer and tongs. The discussion continued, lubricated by copious quantities of His Lordship's finest whiskies until he asked if you were hungry and suggested we have an early breakfast.

Twenty minutes later, a breakfast of fresh orange juice, poached eggs, tea, toast and marmalade made its appearance. You hadn't realised how hungry you were and hoovered up all the food within reach. Looking up you see that that a wan grey light is filtering through the window and look at your watch; 6.30 a.m., the night has flown.

You hear footsteps and the door is flung open with a bang. A large, angry-looking man strides into the room and after fixing the Butler with a furious glare, he turns to point at you and asks who the hell you are? Without waiting for an answer he tells the Butler that he may not bring vagrants back to the house and turns back to you and tells you to get out, now, go!

Shaken, you stand up and head for the door as fast as you can to escape this wrathful apparition. Moments later you stand outside the back door in the Sunday dawn and run down the drive to the main road as fast as you can.

An early morning bus comes past 10 minutes later and you

jump on for the ride to George Square. You walk through the door of your flat, flop down in a kitchen chair with your last cigarette and reflect on a totally surreal night.

You had given him your address and about ten days later you received a letter from him. He had been fired just after you left and promised to keep in touch.

He never did.

THE BOMB THAT WILL BRING US TOGETHER

Margaret Callaghan

THE EXODUS TOOK PLACE in silence; roads empty of traffic, shuttered shops, closed restaurants. Streams of people walked north, south, east and west as though some invisible force was repelling them outwards. Occasionally a noisy bar punctured the calm. Its noise obscene at first growing muted as we walked on.

People cradled mobile phones like babies and carried gym bags on their backs like small children. The lucky ones had swapped their heels for trainers and dangled their shoes in their hands, others limped along beside them, some barefoot. We didn't know how long we'd be walking for.

Most people were alone. Some spoke quietly into their phones but rarely did they speak to each other. This was still London. Years of being shoved into people underground in melting, fainting heat, of being jostled and pushed in shopping streets, of living packed on top of each other; years of long queues to get into clubs, to buy train tickets, to go to the toilet, even sometimes to cross the road, had built up an emotional distance to compensate for the lack of a physical one. Occasionally on my way to work I'd see a person on the tube, presumably a newcomer, lean forward and attempt to engage someone in conversation. The recipient would jump startled, as though one of the adverts that they had been gazing at blankly had come to life.

That morning, on my way to a meeting at the Houses of Parliament, the tube journey had been even more unpleasant than usual; delays on the Victoria line, the Piccadilly line cancelled, restrictions on the Northern line. Rumours reached us of electrical failures as one line after another closed and jams of people swarmed up and down stairs in the packed tunnel seeking an alternative route. I'd pushed a little, terrified as ever of being late, more especially that morning when I knew I had to get into the Houses of Parliament on time and knew that the queues would already have started. I regretted delaying myself by returning a DVD.

Finally we reached Victoria Station where I jumped on a bus to

Westminster, pushing it along with the insides of my stomach, drumming my fingers to get some sense of movement, poised to jump off and wondering if I would be faster running than sitting in this crawling line of buses. When finally we reached my stop I disembarked and ran across the road to Westminster weaving in and out of the traffic to arrive gasping at the top of the queue. As I tried to persuade an impassive policeman to let me skip the security queue I heard a crackle from his radio and the words 'bombers'. It seemed as though we all knew at the same time. The only reaction was the increased volume in the queue's chattering. Little in peaceful prosperous Britain had prepared us for this. We were waiting to be shown how to feel.

Finally I got to the top of the queue. Bags searched, bodies scanned, apologies about the slowness because of 'the situation' and I was in.

Inside the Houses of Parliament, the establishment was going on quite as usual. The speaker of the house, my member of parliament in Glasgow, went past in his robes and silk stockings and I smiled as I wondered if he ever considered wearing them at surgeries in the East End of Glasgow, or at home in private. No-one cancelled meetings. No-one raised their voice. No-one showed any emotions. In between meetings we crowded around television sets in the visitors area, which showed pictures of the outside of the building and told of decisions being made in offices next door. I had a strange sense of pressing my nose against glass to see inside to where I was.

Finally I left the Houses of Parliament and joined the long walk home. I walked up an empty Westminster, past Downing street, empty of photographing tourists, past the closed tubes, past the empty restaurants and cancelled theatre shows of Soho. Without my phone I felt alone and unreal, despite being surrounded by people. There were no comments, no jokes, no feeling that we were in this together.

After a mile or so the occasional bus appeared. I caught one going in the general direction of my house and, as it made its way north, it began to fill up, although the top decks remained empty. Rare taxis picked up individuals. I thought about late night drunken taxi queues in Glasgow, where people would shout the area to which they were going to try to find others going the same way. When we reached Kings Cross we were evicted from the bus and had to walk through alleyways and around housing estates to get past the large area which had been cordoned off, as police and bomb disposal experts searched for evidence.

The next day journalists wrote hand-wringing articles debating whether they should have stopped to offer people a lift, and it amazed me that this was something which they had to think about and scared me that their decision was generally 'no'. That weekend I lay in bed reading the newspapers and realised that on the missing list was someone who had said goodbye to her boyfriend from the same station as me.

By then I had begun to understand. Every year you live in London you add on another layer: of fear, of separateness, of distance, of exhaustion, and as the years go on the layers become you. You close the door to your mind and retreat to the space behind it.

But that day I got home and turned on my mobile. An explosion of texts and answer machine messages. 'Are you OK?' 'Where are you?' I turned on my computer, another 30 e-mails from people from Glasgow: old work colleagues, friends from university, people I could hardly remember. I composed the same text and e-mail. 'I'm fine.'

THE MEANING OF BOONDOGGLE
AND OTHER STORIES

Fraser Edmond

THE DAY IS 20 June 2008.

The day is a Friday.

The day is sunny and warm.

The day is today and, at first glance, today would appear rather depressing.

I wake early, which is a rarity, not due to some fresh flush of inspiration or determinism to do something productive but because today is a workday in the heart of the Edinburgh International Film Festival and overtime is expected. The day is dull, too many unknown staff, not enough work to keep everyone busy. I wait it out with impatience, desperate to leave, to get home with no thought of what I'll do when I get there.

The day is sunny and warm. There are no windows at work, it is 27 degrees inside.

The sun is blinding while walking westwards home at just after five o'clock but the journey doesn't take long.

My wife is home before me, swooning over a 1963 Hillman Minx convertible on eBay that we can't afford but it's pretty and that's all that matters.

After a brief, microwaved dinner and with a stomach that feels like it's plotting something I walk into town to meet a friend. She has to leave early because she is pregnant and tired.

I walk all the way home again.

With the sun setting prettily behind the architecture of Edinburgh I consider picking out a good book, a good beer and, most importantly, a good cushion and heading down to the park at the end of the street but I can't take the thought of dog-walkers and Frisbees and, heaven forbid, children. Instead I settle for a night of insular darkness with a DVD randomly plucked from the ever-growing 'yet to watch' pile. My wife, keen at first, falls asleep on my arm within minutes.

I go to bed early.

The day is 20 June 2008.

This is my day. My day, at first glance, may appear rather depressing but God, as they say, is in the details. It is the minutiae and small moments that bring joy to lives, that lift our souls and carry us through the tedium and monotony. The details of a life cannot be seen at first glance. So let's run through that again, but this time let's focus a little more closely.

Getting up early means the local bakery is still open. Bran flakes for breakfast may be good for the body but doughnuts are better for the soul.

Work is so quiet that no one minds/cares/notices that I take half an hour to sit outside with an ice cream. A pretty girl that I don't know smiles at me as she walks past and unconsciously sways her behind most alluringly as she walks away. On my lunch break I read in the *Metro* newspaper that Roddy Woomble is spearheading a new writing competition and later, as there is a lot of it going on, I learn the meaning of the word boondoggle. Plus, of course, the Film Festival is in town. I love stories in any form they can be presented, thus a two week deluge of new and varied stories from around the world can't fail to be invigorating. Just because this day is dull doesn't mean that those around it are. In my time of tenuous association with the EIFF I have had the opportunity to meet with some of my personal heroes, such as the brain-meltingly talented artist Dave McKean and the delectable Glaswegian actress Laura Fraser. So while I may not exactly love my job, I do love the perks it provides.

On my walk home my eyes may be watering but my face is warm and I feel, if only for a fleeting time, healthy.

My wife, Felicity, who is sprawled across the sofa as I get home, is an incredibly kind, sensitive and easily excitable human being with the soul of a bruised child and the arse of a pageant swimsuit round winner who I love dearly and constantly feel proud to come home to every day (but don't ever tell her I said so, she's also fun to annoy).

And the 1963 Hillman Minx convertible really is a very pretty car. Felicity tells me of her theory that not all cars are, in fact, girls. The 1963 Hillman Minx convertible, for example, is an eight-year-old boy, it wears shorts and likes stickers. It is good to dream.

The friend I meet in town is a local artist and animator with whom everyone I've ever met is secretly in love. We're meeting to discuss ideas for my next tattoo and before she leaves she is able to pass on a series of design sketches for me to peruse at my leisure. They are uniformly beautiful.

I walk all the way home again, listening to the new Dresden Dolls album and smiling.

Yes, I may have a touch of misanthropy in me but why the hell should you care?

As I draw the curtains and settle in for a night of insular, cosy, womb-like darkness, the DVD plucked from the pile turns out to be *Pollock*, a touching biopic of the troubled and controversial painter with whom I've developed a mild fascination over the previous few weeks. Whilst watching it, with Felicity's head on my shoulder and her breath tickling the hairs on my arm, I begin to question the nature of art.

We go to bed early, but this is a common euphemism.

So this is my day, just another one of my days in the long string of my life. A life lived through the art of others. I lie awake and return to my previous thought, just what is art anyway? And as the clock ticks over to 11.59 p.m. an answer comes back. Art is whatever gets you through the day. Movies, music, pretty girls and doughnuts.

The day is 20 June 2008.

The day is now over.

It was a good day.

DINE AND DASH

Graham Forbes

THIRTY, NO, NEARER 40 years on, and I still feel guilty about it. I'm not a criminal, but it was theft and I was the thief. But any time I think about it the guilt quickly dissolves in laughter. It must have looked hilarious.

Och, I was young.

I was a skinny, struggling musician living in a cold bedsit in Hillhead Street. I was playing in a band, it was all I wanted to do and no sacrifice was too great. I could have found myself a job, there was no shortage of easy work in those days, but that was a trap that soon led to a lifetime of toil and abandoned dreams. And the thought of being a part-time musician was horrible. That would have made music a hobby. No. I'd rather starve.

It was a dark, dreich, February night, and neither I nor one of the guys in the band had eaten in two days. It was wet, that misty, soaking Glasgow drizzle, and we were plodding up Gibson Street past the Taj Mahal, then the Koh-i-Noor, then the glorious Shish Mahal, the jewel in the crown of West End curry houses. The sweet, heady aroma of hot sauce reached out to us, oh so terribly, so tantalisingly.

'What I wouldn't give for a lamb biryani,' I said, leaving the thought hanging in the air.

'A prawn vindaloo,' replied my pal.

'A daal gosht would be wonderful,' I mused.

'Or even a poke of pakora.' He licked his lips. He was a drummer; his tastes were simple.

We checked our pockets, but it was pointless even looking – we only needed about 70 pence, but we knew the last of our few coins had long gone on a packet of roll-up tobacco. Some things were more important than food.

Then we saw the Gates; that awful, always empty Indian eatery on Bank Street. No-one in their right mind went to the Gates. Even drunks would rather queue in the rain outside the Shish than eat in the Gates. It had a terrible reputation involving stomach pain and food poisoning. It loitered at the corner, hanging on the coattails of the great names across the street, trying to sponge up the overflow of customers when the other restaurants were packed. Only strangers who didn't know any better entered the Gates.

We went in.

It was empty, as it always was on a dark Tuesday night. The waiter eyed us suspiciously when we chose a table near the door. Too near. He knew what we were up to. But we were starving.

Soon we were drooling over our curries, ripping apart chapattis, making little parcels of yellow-coloured rice and chunky, juicy lamb, gurgling down a jug of cold water – oh, this was so good.

It would be a first for me, but I had it figured out. Timing was everything. We cleared our heaped plates, mopped up the last of the thick sauce with scraps of naan bread and sat back in our chairs. Ahh. We noticed three waiters were now watching us closely, waiting for us to make our move.

'That was excellent,' we said, smiling at our waiter, trying to win him over. I guessed that was something he hadn't heard very often.

'Could we have ice cream with lychees? Oh, and two coffees, please.' I was trying to sound casual, relaxed, but my heart was pounding. Could he hear it? The watching waiters seemed to un-tense slightly, we wouldn't do it until we had finished eating. This was exactly what I wanted them to think.

I whispered to my pal, 'I'm going to the lavvy. As soon as I get back to the table, run.'

I stood and sauntered past the waiter bringing our ice creams and coffees. Went into the toilet. I was sweating. We hadn't a penny between us. We could get arrested for this. I splashed cold water on my face. When I came out, I forced myself to stroll slowly back to our table, so near the door. The waiters watched me; their dark eyes narrow, hostile. I reached the table.

'NOW!'

I yelled it. I mean really yelled. A whisper would have been enough. There was the clatter of plates dropping in the kitchen. Everyone had heard me.

Startled, my pal leapt to his feet, spilling his coffee all over the ice creams, knocking his old wooden chair to the floor. We rushed the few steps to the door. I crashed into it with my shoulder, trying to push it open.

It opened inwards.

I was oblivious to pain as my head clattered off the glass, and ripped the door open. We rushed across Bank Street straight in front of a fast car, which screeched to a halt. The driver leapt out, yelling at us, were we trying to get bloody killed? Then he jumped back as the shouting waiters charged from the restaurant and a big, heavy guy waving a butcher's machete over his head screamed awful unintelligible curses as he raced after us. He was wearing a lavishly stained once-white apron and ripped blue check trousers; he looked like the chef, and seemed to take our sudden departure as a deep personal insult.

It was the crazed look in his eyes that made us sprint impossibly fast, it must have been, but he was on our heels. The chaser closed on the chased. For a moment I could feel his huge hand grip my shoulder, then I heard him gasp for breath and we left him panting and furious far behind us in the dark street.

Outside Kelvinbridge subway station we doubled over with laughter, even though we knew we were wrong, terribly wrong. It might have been the worst restaurant in the West End, but it was the best curry we'd ever tasted.

A DEVIL OF A DAY

Steve Gilhooley

SUNDAY SERMON OVER, baptisms done and dusted, I retired to a local drinking consultants in order to quench the fire and brimstone.

I sported a cropped haircut, Billy Connolly T-shirt, jeans and Doc Martens. My mate, Harry, having just finished his employment, wore a suit. The new owners of the bar didn't allow swearing so we decided to leave to seek out a less 'Christian' pub.

We wandered into The Woodhall Arms. I had heard of George, the ex-footballer proprietor and I assumed that he had heard of me. We had never met though.

The locals nudged George and whispered, 'That's the priest!' George duly breezed over, extended a hospitable hand saying, 'Heard a lot about you, Father Steve,' and proceeded to shake hands with... Harry. Harry politely informed him that I was the anointed one. 'Whit?' George cried, 'I had him doon as a brickie!'

We sat down with George and it wasn't long before he popped the question, 'Tell me, Father, dae ye dae exercises?' Perplexed at his enquiry I informed him that I attended the gym three times a week. 'Naw', he laughed, 'EXERCISES! Gettin rid o' ghosts.' I kept a straight face and told him that I did them all the time. In fact, I had never performed an exorcism in my life.

He explained that his other pub in Leith was haunted and that the bar staff would not go down to the cellar. He invited me to go with him to 'do the business' as he put it.

We arrived and slowly made our way down the winding stairs. The temperature dropped noticeably as we descended. It was so chilly I could actually see my own breath. George fiddled with a set of keys and eventually wrestled the huge oak door open. He tugged on a frayed piece of string and a very dull light bulb fought a losing battle against the darkness in the windowless room.

I stood completely still in the middle of the cellar then slowly extended my arms. George whispered, 'Have you started yet?'

'No,' I whispered back feigning irritation at his interruption, 'I'm just sussing out who's here...or what's here.'

'OK, are you ready, George?' He nodded his head, gulped

nervously and stepped back to the perceived safety of the doorway. God and George only know what he was expecting to unfold. Summoning up all my earthly powers I shouted, 'Ghosts...bugger off!'

George looked shocked and stunned and said disappointedly, 'Is that it? I thought ye were supposed tae say something holy.'

'OK,' I obliged, 'Ghosts, bugger off, Amen.'

With that, I about turned and headed back up the stairs.

George locked the door and followed at my heels, 'Are you sure you're no a brickie?'

Back at the bar he poured me a brandy to calm his nerves. I sunk it in a one-er to which he complained, 'Aye, ye got got rid o' that spirit quickly enough!'

WATERFALL

William Letford

Siobhan Redmond's favourite story

THIS PARTICULAR NIGHT was sometime in the middle of January. No Christmas glamour. No snow. Just January and driving rain. I was trying hard to keep my head up but I was walking straight into the wind. I'm stubborn though. The weather wasn't going to beat me.

Appreciating Scottish weather is all about posture. When the rain belts it down keep your shoulders back and your head high. As soon as your head drops you start to slump and when that happens; you curdle in on yourself. Stand tall.

So that was me, the tall man.

I wasn't dressed for it either. At 19 my wardrobe wasn't the only thing full of vanity and fashion. Warmth and practicality rarely entered my head. You could see my moles through the shirt I was wearing. I came to a compromise. Don't slouch. Don't curdle in on yourself. Slip into a doorway. Wait for the worst of it to pass then ease yourself out as tall as you like.

The first doorway that came my way was the entrance to Oxfam. I sidestepped into it and had to kick a couple of black bags to make room but once I was out of the wind my breath came less shallow. I looked down at the bags.

I knew I wasn't going to steal anything. I only wanted something while I was standing there. One bag was full of board games. The other was full of women's clothes. Useless. I went back to the women's clothes and picked out a cherry-coloured cardigan. The arms didn't reach as far as my wrists but it would do for five minutes.

The gutter across the street was running full. The downpipe was choked so an urban waterfall had formed. It battered against the pavement. A woman came to the waterfall and stepped onto the road to avoid it. She noticed me in the doorway and crossed the street.

Her hands were stuffed into her coat pockets and her shoulders were bunched. I remember she was older than me and I had clocked right away, as you do, that she wasn't attractive but for some reason I stared at her all the way across the road. She came right up to the doorway and crouched down over the black bags. After she had rummaged she stood up and said, 'No umbrella,' she looked at my cardigan, 'but then you could have told me that, couldn't you?'

I hadn't even thought of it. I looked at her again. She still wasn't what I would've called attractive but...there was something. She drew her wet fringe across her forehead, tucked it behind her ear and walked away. Then it hit me.

I was 14. My Uncle had taken me out to work with him for the summer. He was a roofer. We were in the van, driving through town, and a girl I knew from school waved at me. He whistled at the ceiling. 'What about her?' he said to me. 'She's a wee cracker.' I showed him the eyes. 'Uncle Casey,' I said, 'she's roastin.' He pulled in to the side of the road. Stopped the van and turned off the engine. 'Listen, son,' he said, 'when you get older, and if you're lucky, you see different things in girls. They don't always have to look gorgeous. Sometimes they've got lights. You can't see them. They're under the skin but you know they're there.'

Standing in that doorway to Oxfam, 19 years old and wearing a cherry-coloured women's cardigan, I noticed it. The woman that walked away in the rain. She had lights.

HITCHING A LIFT WITH FRED WEST

Felicity Nightingale

I FREQUENTLY HITCHED lifts when I was young and penniless, there was freedom and adventure out there on the highways.

I met a few mad eccentrics on my travels as a single girl, but men, it was usually men – tended to fall into two categories: protective father figures who bought me cups of tea at service stations or the chancers with their sly sexual innuendos.

I was 22 when I had my most peculiar lift, hitching home to Weymouth from Wigan with a scribbled note of places I should pass; Birmingham, Gloucester, Bristol.

I never waited long and after several lifts a kindly lorry driver bought me a cup of tea at a service station near Gloucester. He headed elsewhere and I strolled across the garage forecourt looking ahead for a suitable hitching spot. I noticed a dark blue van parked at the kerbside and as I drew nearer a man crossed the road and approached me. He asked if I was looking for a lift.

I was surprised to be approached but I could see no obvious reason to refuse him. I didn't stop to analyse the peculiarity right then but I didn't like him for it. He wasn't physically threatening but neither was there any pleasantness about him. He was thin with a long face and a high square forehead.

His van was anonymous, tidy and almost empty in the back. I refused to put my rucksack in there, I said I would keep it on my lap.

He then realised he needed a cup of tea. Why should he be parked at the exit before remembering this? I was eager to be on my way but he persuaded me to stay so out of politeness I did.

He insisted on paying for the tea and we sat at a table where he asked me about myself whilst revealing only that he was a builder. He was curious about my family and then aggressively demanded to know what sort of parents would allow their daughter to hitch hike. I explained that they weren't happy but it was my decision. 'Don't they realise how dangerous it is?' he asked, appalled at their lack of concern for me. When I stopped trying to defend them he would calm down.

He told me that I should come back to spend the night with his

123

family in Tewkesbury as it was unlikely that I would reach home before dark now and his wife and children would be delighted. I was welcome to stay longer since my own parents didn't appear to care for me. I contradicted this but it only provoked him. I thanked him and said I needed to get back or my mother would worry.

This put him into a fitful temper again. He demanded to know how I would cope when darkness fell, freezing cold on some lonely road with nowhere to spend the night. I remained confident I'd get home that day.

We returned to his van driving south on the M5. After a while he told me that I was heading the wrong way. This was not the direction for Weymouth, I actually needed to head back towards Tewkesbury.

He explained that he would drop me off here at the roadside so that I could cross to the other side and hitch in the opposite direction. I told him that it was illegal to walk across a motorway. Irritated, he told me this was not a motorway. I insisted it was ('Look, the signs are blue for a motorway!') His anger was intimidating so I stopped being disagreeable.

My mind had started responding to his anger rather than my own common sense.

He told me he had to meet someone on business and would be turning off at the roundabout ahead. He would return home later and if I was still hitching he would pick me up. He made it sound like a favour.

He stopped on the hard shoulder and I remember him unloading my rucksack from the back of the van. I was shocked to be dumped in the middle of a motorway and bizarrely I really did stagger smartly across the four lanes with my luggage on my back where I stuck out my thumb.

A lorry instantly drew up for me.

As I climbed up into the cab the driver asked where I was going. 'Weymouth,' I said.

You're going in the wrong direction for Weymouth,' he said.

'Yes, I know!' I replied.

'It's illegal to hitch on a motorway,' he said.

'Yes, I know!' I replied.

He delivered me back to the service station. It no longer exists but there used to be a connecting footbridge across the motorway.

I continued hitching and eventually arrived home late in the dark.

My mother was in the kitchen with one of my sisters. 'Today I had the strangest lift which doesn't make sense!'

'Oh, well,' they said, 'you got here, didn't you?'

For years I would go over the details trying to work out a reason. The man was humourless; it was hardly a practical joke.

In 1994 Fred West and his wife Rose were found guilty of the torture, rape and murder of young women, nine of whose dismembered bodies were buried beneath the cellar and in their garden in Gloucester, near Tewkesbury.

Reading a summary of the trial in a Sunday paper I came across a picture of a younger Fred. The man I had had a lift with that day.

Finally the mystery was solved. He must have intended to turn around, pick me up and drive me to his home.

Drivers wouldn't normally stop along a motorway so he would have expected me to be grateful, maybe greeting him with familiarity. Possibly he did turn off to meet a business acquaintance who could later have testified that the van was empty.

I would have last been seen hitching south.

TWO KINDS OF BUS PASSENGER

Keira Oliver

THERE ARE TWO KINDS of people in this world. The first would never ever get on public transport in a million years. The other has to grin and bare it. I'm in the latter camp. Standing in a line of equally depressed people desperate to get home, I pray for the bus to arrive. To make matters worse, today the rain is pelting off the road like it's trying to give it a facelift. And worse again, it's Edinburgh in August.

Locals tend to handle the Festival in one of two ways. The first is to embrace it, take time off work, and eagerly drink overpriced beer while watching overrated comedians. The rest try to ignore it as best they can. I am the latter.

As I wait impatiently, I curse myself for not renting out my flat to some Bangkok Ladyboys so I could escape to the Caribbean where there would be sun and I would be the tourist. However, I have a survival plan (for the bus journey anyway) and congratulate myself on how cunning and clever it is. I've discovered a bus route that totally misses out Princes Street: the artillery road that, at this time of year, is so chock-full of tourists looking for the right change and directions to the castle (it's behind you) that it would give any Edinburgher a heart attack.

Shockingly, I realise that my secret is out when the bus arrives bursting with wet tourists, babbling Spanish students and harassed office workers. As soon as I get on board, I wilt like a daisy in a hothouse, and hope, against all odds, for a vacant seat before I faint.

As every Scot knows, there is a certain etiquette to follow as a bus passenger (not that the first group would know this, lucky gits). I like to think that I conduct myself with some decorum: never, ever, sitting next to someone, or even behind them, unless I absolutely have to and offering my seat to an old person (occasionally they look like you've just slapped them in the face, giving you evils all the way home for implying that they're too old to handle standing up). However, all sense of propriety goes out the window when the bus is heaving like this one. While the people in front of me shuffle up the bus, I nab an overlooked seat next to a woman with a pushchair.

Now this is an issue that definitely divides the city. Either you think that the elderly, the infirm, people with luggage, ridiculous numbers of Sainsbury's bags, buggies and all children should be banned from travelling, or you think that they have as much right to be there as the rest of us. Of course, I'm the latter.

The woman next to me looked like she could weep for inconveniencing everyone with her buggy. Her baby however was completely oblivious and beamed enthusiastically at all his fellow passengers. Smiling babies also tend to divide the nation. The first suddenly become very interested in the adverts above them for Debt Hotlines, while the others can't help but smile back. And maybe stick out their tongues playfully at them. I, of course, am the latter.

After a few minutes of swapping smiles, I realised that something else was going on on that bus. Something strange. This was unlike any bus I had ever been on. Normally, despite being full, the bus is silent (except maybe the git on a mobile deciding what to wear at the weekend). People stick their headphones in, read their book or stare out the window: anything rather than inadvertently catch someone's eye. But looking around, it was like the worst of the weather had brought out the best in my fellow passengers.

I noticed that people were talking to each other. The young mum struck up a conversation with me (to be honest it was a welcome distraction from the woman who was pressing her breasts into the side of my head). A well-dressed man was asking a tourist what he thought of Edinburgh and they joked that this was the closest they had been to any locals since they had arrived. Two women who hadn't seen each other in years suddenly started waving and trying to catch up over everyone's heads. When a man got on the bus and tried to use his staff pass instead of his bus pass, people actually laughed with him. And then the strangest thing of all happened.

There are two kinds of bus passenger. The first do not speak to anyone for anything, while the other will at least thank the bus driver for the trip. I am the latter. I think it's only courteous. But I don't think I've ever seen anything like this. Half of the bus had been taken up by a load of Spanish kids here to 'learn English' (please, they speak it better than most natives and look smugly at everyone as if to say 'I could swear right in your face in three different languages and you wouldn't even know it.' Hats off to them, I say.) Two stops before mine, all of them got off and, I kid you not, every single one of them thanked the bus driver. It was an astonishing five minutes.

When I got off at my stop, I'll admit that I was relieved to be escaping the humid air and smell of baby sick, but I left with a smile on my face (after thanking the driver, who smiled and said I was welcome: will wonders never cease?) I can't put my finger on what happened on that bus, but I do know that there would be two kinds of bus passenger on it. The first wouldn't recognise that journey for the uplifting, extraordinary experience that it was. While the second would go on to tell others of what had happened to them. I, of course, am the latter.

THE BALLOON

Carolyn Scott

THE SKY WAS PURPLE – a violet shade almost. It looked mystical, and like something out of a fairytale or cartoon. Childish. It glowed with warmth that brought calm and security amid the cool winter morning. The clock read 7.00 a.m.; I did not quite know how I had awoken. My head was empty apart from the occasional recollections of distant dreams. The details of the night before came to me slowly – a slideshow upon my eyelids, a soundtrack tapping on my eardrums.

I had to be at work by 8.30 a.m. and was rather sure my head had not hit the pillow until at least 4.00 a.m., yet the exact details of the evening before were still held in a misty memory. I felt surprisingly alert, and for a while lay still and calm, held by the purple glow, letting the slideshow roll on and the soundtrack continue to beat.

The colour of the sky was slowly transformed, as if a drop of pink dye had been injected into the dawn air, moving slowly over the vast clear expanse of the atmosphere. It reminded me of watching old chemistry experiments at school, watching as a drop of one substance would slowly combine with another to fill the dusty beaker with new vibrant colours. Just as this memory was forming in my mind, something briefly caught my eye and pulled me from nostalgia. It was quick and darting, I was not sure if it was a creation of my own mind. A whirling movement of bright red flashing across the sky. The sudden motion, juxtapositioned against its calm, now pinkening, background brought me to my senses and I clambered my way out of the warm cocoon my duvet had created.

As I walked down Blair Street the sun was just beginning to light the tops of the ancient Edinburgh buildings. I have always loved the way the sun slowly made its way down the old bricks one row at a time, each row waiting patiently in slumber to be awoken by the delicate heat of the sun's rays.

I enjoy my little walks, standing on the shadows of my own feet, the sun on my back, watching the shadows get smaller and smaller until they disappear under my odd shoes. That childlike battle to catch your own shadow. I drew my attention away from my feet as I approached my favourite part of this regular journey.

I turned round looking down the street and watched the sun rise fully, lighting the distant sea that could just be seen between the ancient buildings of the Royal Mile. The colours on this particular morning seemed more vivid and entrancing than usual. Just as I was falling deep into my own imagination something once again caught my eye and pulled me quickly and abruptly from my little dreamland. Just as before, I couldn't quite tell what it was, a dashing movement of bright, vibrant red.

I turned quickly, looking up into the now turquoise sky. As I turned the sun hit my eyes and shot through my head. When my vision returned, and the bright dots darting across my eyes like flying saucers faded, I finally saw what it was that had startled me – on two occasions now!

Dancing erratically across the sky, held afloat by the typical Edinburgh winds I had grown to adore was a little red balloon, pulling behind it a shiny white cord.

The sight of it created within me the most spectacular variety of emotions; excitement, awe, wonderment, nostalgia and that great sense that there was magic in the air. It reminded me of being a child, going to fairs and highland shows. I would always beg my parents to buy me a 'magic balloon that could float like the clouds' and after five joyful minutes I would release the silky string from my tight youthful grasp to watch as it danced across the sky to join those floating, marshmallow clouds. But for a brief moment I felt a slight sadness.

As a child I had loved to release these plastic bubbles of gas into the wind and watch them rise, but was always aware of the honest sadness so many other children experienced as they lost their grasp on that silky string and watched their prized possession disappear into the unknown. Its fate decided by the perplexing winds flowing over the land. I thought that this balloon that had now pulled me into its motion could well be one of those prized possessions that had escaped from a small, sad, sweaty hand. I still couldn't help but smile though, there was something mesmerising about the way this balloon moved.

As it bobbed along George IV Bridge, guided by the top of the library, I found myself following it, eyes fixed on its sway.

I walked staring to the sky, on an adventure, a chase, my adventure. I tried hard to use my peripheral vision to avoid the dangers of lamp-posts, bus stops and the morning commuters who would occasionally glance at me, puzzled, as I walked slowly eyes pinned on the balloon. I followed the balloon down into the Meadows and found myself a bench in the sun on which to rest for a moment. I lit up a cigarette and laid my head back watching the balloon dance above me for a while. As I stubbed the cigarette out on the heel of my shoe the balloon began its ascent, shrinking slowly into the sky. I lay there for a while before strolling through the Meadows to work.

For the rest of the day I smiled, nostalgia crept in and warm memories formed endlessly and stayed with me until I lay my head down to sleep that evening.

LONG WINTER, LONG AFTERNOON

Bill Sutherland

IT WAS, APPARENTLY, a harmless little prank to entertain our little corps of half a dozen guys working in the stores department of a garage in Glasgow during the long, cold February of 1963, which remains one of the worst winters in living memory. Frank was normally a good-natured guy who chatted away; quite the thing with us late-teen and 20-something colleagues. So, it being my turn that day to make the lunchtime cuppa for everyone to go with our packed lunches, what harm was there in having a wee bit of fun by putting some salt in Frank's tea?

He coughed and spluttered and swore. Everybody laughed except Frank, who continued to mutter his favourite swearwords even as I returned from the sink in the corner which served as a kitchen, bringing over a consolation cuppa, already prepared and this time properly made with his customary spoonful of sugar. But Frank was not amused, not happy at all. 'You're gonnae be very, very sorry you did that,' he said in a convincingly serious tone, initially ignoring the fresh cuppa.

'Come on – it's only a joke,' I chuckled. 'There's another cup anyway.'

He brushed me away and insisted: 'I don't care. You're for it. You're really for it.'

I walked away with a shrug in the way that you do when someone is in a serious huff with you and I began to chat with some of the other guys. Whenever I thought Frank wasn't looking, I would sound out their opinions about what form his retaliation might take and the consensus was that it would not be anything to worry about, nothing serious anyway, although nobody had any suggestions about what it might be.

And so back to work, dealing with customers at the counter, checking the stock lists for what they wanted, and fetching the appropriate car or van parts from the store ledges. When I wasn't busy, and frequently even when I was, my thoughts would return to this unknown punishment which awaited me between now and closing time, a few hours away. Or maybe later. 'Nothing to worry about?' Hmm, I wouldn't say that exactly.

But the offence wasn't that bad, was it? Maybe it was just the indignity of people laughing at him. Whatever, it was hardly the crime of the century so surely the punishment couldn't be that big a deal. I reasoned that I could rule out anything violent, although he might have decided on some silly prank to play on me. What could it be? I tried to think of what I might do if I were in his place. There was fresh snow lying on the ground outside…

Maybe it could be narrowed down to something he could do on his own? Maybe not, so I tried to watch if he had any secretive-looking chats with any one. Anyone of the guys who had had a good laugh earlier might now think it was fair game to even it up by helping him out at my expense. By speaking to everyone in turn I thought I might get some clues or suggestions. Everyone was not just a pal but a suspect now. Perhaps a potential accomplice might trip himself up and give the game away.

Having made no progress that way I decided to tackle the man himself. 'So you're not going to tell me what this thing is that you're going to do to get back at me?' I asked with an affected mixture of self-assurance and impatience. 'No,' he replied, impassive. 'Okay. Big deal,' I answered irritably as I walked away, feigning nonchalance.

The stores foreman, an approachable older man named Guy was no help either. 'Frank wouldnae dae anybody any harm!' he pointed out by way of reassurance. No real harm. Nothing serious. Yes, yes, I knew he was not going to break my legs, but what could it actually be?

Later, I caught Frank's eye and smiled over at him. His response was to carry on with what he was doing before looking back at me and running his finger across his throat in mock-Mafia fashion. Two or three times, just to make sure I had got the message. That seemed to make light of it but didn't really help much, as I was already totally convinced by now that, whatever it was, it wouldn't be too serious…yes, but what?

As the seemingly stationary clock reluctantly reached one hour from the dreaded five o'clock, I was finally left to work things out on my own when Wee Gary, probably my closest friend, told me he had had enough of this as a topic of conversation. 'Gonnae gi'e us peace, Bill? Please! Don't know what Frank's gonnae dae, a' right? Nae idea. Ye've been nippin' ma heid aboot this a' afternoon.'

It was all very well for him to shrug it off. I continued to worry, of course, but my mood gradually became one of resignation rather than curiosity. That transition also focused me on a plan – to get ready for a quick getaway at five o'clock. Yes, that would be a help! He would first have to catch me...

When the time came I grabbed my coat and looked over my shoulder for Frank, expecting him to make a move or at least follow closely behind me towards the door. Instead, he was seated, looking totally relaxed.

'Goodnight, Bill,' he said, smiling this time. I looked puzzled and asked: 'What about the punishment you were going to do?'

'Me? I'm no' gonnae dae anything,' chuckled Frank. 'I don't need to. You've obviously been worried about it all afternoon, and that's good enough for me.' I then gave the fleeting smile of the mightily relieved and unexpectedly reprieved.

'That was the point,' he explained. 'I think it was Franklin Roosevelt who said: "We have nothing to fear except fear itself." Something like that anyway. See you tomorrow, Bill.'

Everybody laughed except me.

Tough Times

THE CHRISTMAS CONCERT

Angus Binnie

JACK, A FRIEND OF MINE, is an Assistant Governor at our local prison. When I met him in the street one December day some years back, he handed me a printed ticket. It was an invitation for two to the prisoners' Christmas Concert.

'Hope you and your wife will come, it's good fun if a bit rough and ready, just remember to bring earplugs, you'll really need them, no kidding.'

He went off leaving me clutching the ticket and contemplating his 'health warning'. My wife and I attended all right but we went without any form of ear protection, not having taken seriously the advice Jack had given.

The concert blasted off to a rousing start and thereafter raged along at a furious pace. There were rude jokes, raucous remarks and crude sketches, each one aimed at wounding every authority figure in sight. All the short sketches were interspersed with deafening music and songs from prisoners' pop groups, each one outdoing the one before in both volume and questionable musicality. There was no doubt the prisoners were doing their level best to provide a memorable and fun occasion for their captive audience. Though I had to firmly remind myself often not to be over-critical of their efforts, it being the season of goodwill and all that, after all.

At least the performers, if not their audience, were certainly enjoying their one night of the year when they could indulge openly in a spot of anarchy and mayhem. There was no denying the roof of the hall was being raised and we were none too happy about the walls holding out either. How we regretted not taking Jack's advice as we both would have appreciated earplugs now. Looking around the hall, some others had also developed a dazed look, best translated as – 'why did we let ourselves in for this?' and by the halfway stage we were almost prepared to wave white hankies in surrender. One prisoner even managed to do a streak on stage for a second or two, though the dignitaries and their ladies in the front row whooped and laughed with the rest of us.

Towards what we now fervently hoped would soon be the end

of the concert, the hall and stage darkened completely and an uncanny silence descended. A single spotlight suddenly pierced the blackness to pick out one man in white shirt, black bow tie, white jacket, white trousers, motionless in profile with a silver trumpet to his lips...then, in the clearest, sweetest tones imaginable, the Christmas Carol, 'Silent Night! Holy Night!', was played to perfection. I was thankful not to be wearing ear plugs as this was a very moving and unexpected event. It seemed to affect everyone.

However, for me, the effect was absolutely dramatic as I found myself transported in time, carried back across the years to the Second World War and in the front line on Christmas Eve 1944. We were facing a German Panzer Division.

Our platoon, defensively spread out around Kreuzrath village just inside the German border, had had hopes of being out of the front line for Christmas and New Year, but it was not to be. Fortunately, there had been little or no activity by the Germans other than some patrolling although our own artillery, having overlooked the fact it was Christmas time, constantly pounded their forward positions and supply lines. When the rumble from our big guns finally died away around 11.00 a.m., there seemed nothing for it but to stay alert, listen and watch, knowing the enemy to be only some 300 yards out from our trenches and fox holes.

It was cold, the ground icy and snow covered. Before midnight, the peace was broken by a German soldier shouting to us in a friendly voice, 'Halloo Tommee, halloo Tommee.' No one responded, we had strict orders to stay silent and not react. He shouted again, got no response but his halloos were soon followed by the unmistakable notes of a silver trumpet, playing...'Stille Nacht, Hiel'ge Nacht', 'Silent Night! Holy Night!'

It sounded clear and beautiful coming across 'no-man's-land' to swamp every one of us in a sea of nostalgia. There was a great yearning amongst us to be home with our families and to be away from war. The carol hung for ever it seemed on the still, frosty air, never to be forgotten, never to be repeated, but now, all these years later, here it was again.

My friend, Jack, the Assistant Governor, told me afterwards that the trumpet player was a German chap but that fact came as no surprise to me.

THE FIRST CUT IS THE DEEPEST

Noel Connolly

A DAY THAT WILL be forever etched in my psyche is 6 August 1998, the day I got the 'snip'. At exactly 10.30 a.m. that morning I found myself taking a seat with my wife in a worryingly quiet waiting room alongside another eight condemned men. I tried to quell my rising panic by indulging myself in one of the many brochures left on the nearby coffee table, informing me how painless and easy the procedure was and how professional and caring the staff were. But the only thing I was worried about was getting a surgeon with cold hands.

I had only had to wait for around 10 minutes, (the longest 10 minutes of my life) when my name was called out by the receptionist. With some assistance from my better half I managed to prise my fingernails from the arms of the chair and disengage my feet from around the chair legs, and made my way slowly out of the door, where I was to meet the man who was going to alter the way I walked for the next couple of weeks.

With an uncanny resemblance to the cartoon character Professor Calculus from *Tintin*, the surgeon proffered his hand and gave a polite 'hello'. I took his clammy but warm hand, and mumbled 'hello' back in a little boy's voice. He showed me into a small room with nothing in it apart from a surgical table, a trolley weighed down with an assortment of vicious looking medical instruments on it, a changing screen in one corner and several chairs in another. Please God, I thought, I hope no one's coming in to spectate.

Politely the 'nutty' Professor asked me to go behind the screen where I was to 'strip up to the waist'. (Why this sudden need for privacy, when a few minutes from now I would come out with all my manly bits fully on display, I couldn't work out, but I did as I was told anyway). Emerging shamefaced, I was told to 'hop on to the table'. Easier said than done. If I tried clambering onto the table freestyle, with everything loose, I could end up having a nasty accident involving my gentleman's sporran. Equally if I had held onto the problematic area one-handed and attempted to climb up, I could very easily have lost my balance and ended up on the floor. I decided to opt for the Ladyboy technique. This involved tucking everything between my thighs as best I could and rolling onto the table with as much decorum as I could muster.

Having made it on the table in one piece, I physically flinched when the surgeon came towards me with a huge hypodermic needle. Like a fool I tugged up the sleeve of my shirt in preparation for an injection in my arm. With my eyes closed I failed to notice that the needle was actually heading much further south, towards my scrotum, plunging efficiently into, firstly my right testicle, and then my left. (I can't describe the pain I felt, I think I've blocked the memory from my mind, but I do still have the teeth marks on my right hand to remind me).

I was informed by this sadist that the anaesthetic 'would take about five minutes to kick in'. But what seemed like mere nanoseconds later he had scalpel in hand and was now carving my scrotum open like a Sunday roast. Again I had to wimp out and look away. The only sensation I could feel was a slight tugging, which I guessed were the tubes being pulled into a position to be severed. I heard two clear snips, from a pair of surgical scissors. (I hope they were scissors and not something he'd been using to prune his roses the weekend before).

As I lay there praying for time to pass quickly, a peculiar smell entered my nasal passages, like someone was having a fry-up, I could distinctly make out a strong whiff of bacon. Professor Calculus must have clocked me sniffing the air, as he casually informed me that the smell of burning was him 'cauterizing the ends of the tubes, to prevent them from fusing back together'.

A moment later he informed me with a look of glee on his face that 'everything had gone well'. All he had to do now was put in a few stitches, and quickly got to work with a large sewing needle (which I didn't think was necessary to show me), and started suturing my tattered bag with all the skill of a small kid in a trainer factory. 'All done!' he said chirpily as he slapped something cold and smelly onto his handiwork to sterilize the wound.

A rush of air came out of my lungs as I breathed a huge sigh of relief. I thanked the Professor with the same kind of enthusiasm that a freed hostage reserves for his homicidal captor. I now felt I had a bond with this man, having come through such a harrowing experience together, like a kind of manly respect. I don't think the Professor shared the same feelings though. So far he hasn't called, hasn't written, no e-mails, nothing.

LAST DAY IN MAY

Nina Davie

I HADN'T EXPECTED to see her that day but there she was cycling up the hill, Annie; my best friend, confidante and all-round partner in crime.

It was a perfect May morning, bright blue skies, tarmac warm beneath my wheels. I hadn't seen her at first, too busy watching the shadows cast by the bike and me.

'Hi, Annie, how's you?' As soon as the words came out, I caught her eye and knew something was wrong; she'd stopped cycling up hill and was lifting her leg over the bar of her gents bike.

'What's up, Annie?' I tried to sound as casual as ever but this time something told me this was different. There were times when she seemed so fragile yet there were other times when her strength amazed me. I dropped my bike and moved over to where she'd crumpled onto the path. I wrapped my arms around her and gently lifted Annie to her feet. Both our bikes lay abandoned, discarded for now.

'It's just the same old crap, Neen, but I don't know how much more I can take of it.' She was shaking with despair. Her shoulders felt smaller than usual, thinner and I tried to will some strength into her. Recharge her and let her know how much I cared.

'Come on, Annie, why don't we get the bikes together and go for a pedal somewhere nice? A wee bit of the old DIY therapy, and I've got money for a pick-me-up.' She looked up and tried a smile and for a brief second I saw the other Annie shining through. 'Thanks, Neen, I could really do with that. Just what I need.'

Side by side we cycled off to the shop then back down the hill towards Wardie Bay and the beach. 'Glad I bumped into you today, Annie.' I was upbeat as we raced faster and faster downward.

At the beach we dumped our bikes onto the coal speckled sand and using our jackets for blankets, sat down side by side, ready to set her world to right.

It was quite unusual for me to be drinking at this time of day. Barely lunchtime and here I was, about to abandon my world for hers. We'd grown so close over the years. We'd known each other for so long that I couldn't remember the first time we'd met. It was as if it had just always been.

So here we were sitting together looking out at the Firth o' Forth and it glistened back at us, our very own mirror listening quietly to our secrets.

Huddling together, I let Annie know how special she was, not just to me but to everyone she knew. But she was more special to me. She was always there, my thought for the day. I talked of all the good things; her son, her future plans and how I'd be there to help bring them to fruition.

'I love you, Neen.' She said, still staring out at the water.

'You know I've been there Annie and it will get better. It does get better. We learn how to cope over time. Trust me.' Her head lay on my shoulder and I hoped beyond hope that she believed me.

'What about the gorgeous day? And we have this all to share just us and the beautiful sea.' I didn't mention that the tide had turned and was slowly creeping up the beach. Maybe she could see it, already knew.

'We've so much to live for, Annie, and remember, you promised to teach me to drive.

As our pick-me-up started to take effect Annie did cheer up and we began laughing, laughing at it all, all the things that impede our lives, even the incoming tide. We hugged and giggled like school girls playing truant.

Ever so slowly the sun began to sink over the breakwater and we began moving our position upward towards the large sea wall to escape the incoming tide.

Then the inevitable question, 'Time to go I suppose? But we'll be doing this again SOON!'

It was time to get back to reality. But we could cope now. I hugged her and I felt good. Good about myself. Good about her and grateful for this day when I could be there for Annie, as she had so many times for me. It was great to see her smiling as she waved goodbye holding her bike unsteadily with her other hand.

I called to her as she walked up her garden path. 'I'll pop up in the morning. Think we might need a coffee. Love you loads!'

We never had that coffee. The next morning Annie was dead. Found curled up at the end of her bed and all that is left is our yesterday.

CLACKMANNAN TOWER

Corinne Fowler

Jamie Andrew's favourite story

THEY WERE WATCHING and waiting for me back home. Later they told me that Zoe had sat at the attic window twisting long strands of hair and trying to work out what time I'd left. That my mother had sipped black tea without tasting it. And that Jeff insisted I was only taking a walk. But he hid the baby clothes at the back of the airing cupboard and lifted the cot into the attic.

I just wandered. Long strands of hair clung to my neck. I didn't scan the wood for startled deer. Not on that day. I reached the stone bridge and paused to stare into the Black Devon. Then I set out towards Clackmannan tower. I went lurching up the hill towards the barbed wire fence. As I walked, the fingernails of my right hand scraped tufts of wool from the pockets of my sweater. My left hand rasped against the trees' red bark. I saw the tower piercing the ridge ahead.

When I looked back, the trees were steaming like a herd of animals in the open fields. The ground was oozing mud. I stood flicking the bark and dirt from my fingers. The rain was pelting against my scalp, sliding down my cheeks. I put my hands back into the woollen pockets. They were soggy. I took them out again, breathing across the numb skin, stretching out my fingers. At least I'd had the presence of mind to wear my walking boots. I strode uphill towards the tower.

But there was a cold, dead weight curled up inside me. The mud lapped at my boots as I jabbed them into the flabby belly of the hill. The entire slope was liquefying. Marooning me. As I climbed, the view peeped beyond the horizon.

When I reached Clackmannan tower, I clung onto the sandstone blocks while the snow-crested hills heaved and fell about me. I craned my neck upwards. There were clouds spilling over the turrets. My hands dropped to my sides, but I knew I had to keep moving. I started walking. Slowly at first, but soon I was running along the bony spine of the ridge, laughing and laughing. Before I knew it, I was chasing myself round and round the tower, my feet skating over the mud.

Coming to an unsteady halt, I blinked at my mud-spattered clothes and flopped onto my back. The whole tower was spinning out of control, the gargoyles leaning and leering, the giant blocks of stone looking as though they were about to tumble. At first I wanted them to crush me. I rolled onto my belly. The rain drummed onto my head. I tasted grit in my mouth but didn't spit it out, just laid my head against the shuddering ground. The landscape was all smeared, the rain-flattened grass seeping into the curve of the hill, the blades of grass plastered against the horizon the way hair clings to the head of a newborn baby. And while I buried my face in the black soil, the rain slowed and the down-turned mouth of a rainbow appeared above the wood.

I picked myself up and stumbled over to the engraved plaque beneath a snarling pair of gargoyles. 'Clackmannan tower,' I read, 'passed onto the son of Robert the Bruce.' Everyone in history has had a child, I thought. I watched my breath warming the gathering chill. Soon, surely, there would be space for something else. When I was healthy again. Time for thinking about something else.

I knew I wouldn't get lost on the way back. But I had to hurry. My family would be really worried when they found my unmade bed and the empty house. I was bound to look a sight too; pallid, mud-splattered, hunted. I could clean up in the river or, better still, sneak past them into the bathroom and shout cheerfully from the shower. I turned towards the fading bars of colour arching above the trees. The woods were darkening like a bruise.

The barbed wire caught my thigh as I swung over the fence. When I stooped under some low branches, droplets of rain came rolling down the back of my neck. I pulled the heavy wool sweater around me and groped my way through mud and branches. I leaned against a tree for a moment. The hospital had told me to rest. I felt a little dizzy. And the cut from the barbed wire was stinging. I retraced my steps to the river. Then there was a quick crash and snap of twigs and some muffled thuds against fallen branches. I whipped round. Four red deer flashed through the wood. I stared after them until they faded to specks of blackness.

Ahead the stones of the bridge were glistening in the dark. Half way across the bridge I heard the soft hoot of an owl. I paused to wait for the answering call before leaving the wood. I pulled my wet hair back into a pony tail and headed back to the unworn baby clothes, the hidden cradle. I thought, so this is what it's like to walk in the dark. I'd feared and dreaded it for so long. Nearly everyone dreads it. Once night falls, every tree stump becomes a crouching figure. But now I'd left the wood, the estuary came into view. I could see right across the water's rain-puckered surface to the oil refinery at Grangemouth on the far shore. And its lights were flickering like fireflies in the dark.

WHEN REMEMBRANCE BECAME PERSONAL

Neil Griffiths

IMAGINE THE SCENE: Hong Kong in the mid-1970s, I'm on gate duty at my barracks, dwarfed by big dirty blocks of flats and the sun is beating down. Chinese pensioners totter past beneath heavy loads. At 18, I'm tall, slim, and, like all young soldiers, know everything. I'm just about to finish a two-hour stint at the barrier and am looking forward to a cup of tea.

My reverie was broken by two old ladies, Americans obviously, in wing-mirror glasses, trainers and floppy hats. 'We're here to see your chapel, young man,' said one. I looked dumbly back before shouting up to the Provost Sergeant, who was leaning on the guardroom railings above: 'Sergeant, two Americans want to see the chapel!'

'Canadians, we're Canadians!' hissed the lady.

'Well, Griffiths, why don't you show them it? It's time for your relief anyway.' For a second I stood in open-jawed bewilderment. Why should I take Canadians to the chapel? I'm not a tourist guide.

The ladies looked both tired and weak. Sure that my imposing presence, all six foot of military might, would intimidate them, I tried to put them at ease but was firmly put in my place. They had cleared this with the Governor himself, had a letter from His Excellency too, and had spoken personally with my commanding officer, so stop being patronising and show us to the chapel forthwith.

Crestfallen, I showed them the way. 'We're here to visit the memorial plaque to my husband which, I'm assured, hangs in your chapel,' one of them snapped. It seemed that her husband had been one of those shipped over here in 1941 just in time for the Japanese to throw them into a horror camp.

The Canadians had trustingly sent a couple of untrained battalions, young lads, to Britain's aid and the arrivals never had time to do more than march into captivity. I had read about the fall of Hong Kong and the brave, needless and tragic sacrifice. Indians, Gurkhas and other troops had all disappeared at the same time.

My two ladies seemed at least mollified that I had at least an idea of the history and brightened up a wee bit in the erroneous belief that I was a fully briefed guide. I wasn't even sure where the chapel stood. There was a church of sorts but it was too new to have survived the war. Too ashamed to ask anyone, I gambled and took them there.

Fortunately, I was correct. As we entered the cool of the building, the first thing we saw was a gigantic memorial tablet inscribed with a list of names in gold lettering. The husband's name, a Scottish one, was right in the middle. Breathing a quiet sigh of relief, I wondered why I had imagined that the church would have to have been pre-war.

The sound of small sobs awoke me from my self-centred reverie. Quiet tears were rolling down the ladies' crumpled cheeks, their eyes brimming with pain of a loss that they had never forgotten. Suddenly they were small, bent old women, lost in grief. Old folk crying is a terrible thing and I was torn between muteness and words of comfort. They must have known full well what the husband had gone through, but now they were proud and moved to see his name chiselled in stone in this faraway land.

'You must think us real old fools,' said one, wiping away a tear. 'But just to see this; you'll never know and I hope you won't have to.'

Her friend was more in control and grasped my hand. 'And you, young man, must tell us all about your life here!' Her face unfolded in forced humour. The other nodded, smiling slowly. I was suddenly their link with the past, as a young soldier in Hong Kong, living where her husband had once lived. Animated now, and without the previous imperiousness (which I now knew to be a front) they had been steeling themselves, they wanted to know everything about me. I began humbly, but within minutes was outlining my heroic existence on such a shameless scale that I was nearly claiming outright command of the regiment. Their eyes shone and I realized that, if nothing else, they were cheering up.

'You know, we haven't thought to ask your name.'

'Neil Griffiths.'

'Well, Neil Griffiths, you've been real helpful and I want you to take this,' she said, offering a $10 bill.

'I can't!' I hissed, half shocked and half wondering how much it was worth. 'Just tell the sergeant that I was really helpful.' We strolled back to the guardroom.

'The kid's been real helpful, how about giving him a half day off?' The Provost Sergeant grinned serenely but replied that helpfulness was all he would expect from a member of the regiment but Griffiths was just too valuable to disappear right now. The ladies giggled and beamed. 'Well, we tried. Many thanks and goodbye.' I waved back like a grandson, blushing at the snorts behind me, but I had gained my first insight into remembrance and what it means, a message that still rings across the years.

THE MIRACLE IN THE WINDY GOWL

Vicki Jarrett

It's a bright blue spring day in Edinburgh in 1986. I'm 18 years old and reckon I'm living the life. I was wrong about quite a lot of things then.

Since leaving home six months ago, I've been exploring all the dangers the adult world has to offer. My latest project is a massive biker with dirty hands and a bad attitude. He's exactly the sort of man any parent would want their daughter to avoid, hence the attraction. The shouting and swearing rows are a new thing after living with my quietly-spoken parents. Despite the novelty, I don't really enjoy them. I wonder if this is how people who aren't my parents are supposed to behave. How should I know?

This morning we're going with a bunch of friends to Knockhill to watch the racing and leave the flat at the top of Leith in a group of around half a dozen bikes, some carrying pillions. We've already had a row and we're both driving angry, glaring at each other at every set of lights.

I have my own bike, no pillion nonsense for this grown-up, independent woman. We tear up towards the Queen's Park, the sunshine and warmth presenting an unmissable opportunity to throw the bikes round the bends on the lower Duddingston Road before heading out of town to the joys of the Coast Road. We enter the park and take the low road.

Past Hangman's Rock like a great, black lump of coal. Round past Samson's Ribs, red and exposed like old meat. Everywhere the landscape is scattered with gorse and windblown grasses. The sky is china blue with soft brush strokes of cloud. Seagulls hang in the air over the park like tiny white kites.

Since I've not passed my test yet, I have a small bike: a blue hornet-like trail bike with skinny, knobbly tires. I try to keep up with the bigger road bikes but I'm soon trailing in last place. Not that it's a race, but who wants to be last all the same?

I'm going way too fast as I pull the bike into a sharp left and hurtle down into the shadowy, wind-blasted cleft of the Windy Gowl. I'm hugging the bike into the bend, left knee perilously close to the rock, praying for the road to straighten out but the bend keeps on tightening. I already know I'm not going to make it when my front wheel hits a drain cover and folds in on itself, catapulting me high into the blue spring sky.

I think several pointless thoughts one after another: 'Wow, time really does slow down', 'Oh crap, I'm going to die', and 'Sorry, Mum'. I'm almost hovering, suspended within a split second that feels much longer. I see Duddingston Loch below me to the right shining like a mirror. I can see clouds floating in it. I notice that I'm level with a seagull. It turns its sleek white head and eyes me sceptically.

Then I'm down hard and rolling over and over. I see my bike pogoing down behind me, crashing down onto its front wheels, the forks contracting and hurling it back into the air. Somehow it comes down on my right shin and bounces off again and we continue our crashing descent separately. It seems to last forever, a kaleidoscope of vivid images: rock and gorse, tarmac, sky, rock, tarmac, gorse, sky, twirling round and round.

When I eventually come to a halt all I feel is angry – angry at myself, angry at the drain cover, angry at him, angry that my bike's smashed. There's so much anger I don't know what to do with it and start punching the hill, spitting curses into my helmet.

A couple come running over, asking if I'm hurt. How should I know? Then another older guy runs up, he's a doctor and is asking lots of questions. A police car turns up and an ambulance whizzes round the corner. I'm starting to wonder if these people were all following me, waiting for this to happen. Oh, and there he is, must have noticed eventually that I wasn't behind him anymore. I'd rather he went away. He does.

I'm being urged into the ambulance. My leg starts to hurt. A guy with a huge pair of scissors insists on cutting my jeans open from the ankle to the thigh. I'm trying to stop him: they're my best jeans. The leg is looking big but intact. I notice that bits of the skin on my forearms are missing and my left elbow isn't feeling quite right now I come to think about it.

At the hospital they insist on putting me in a series of wheeled things and referring to me as This Young Lady. I reckon they're being sarcastic but I'm in no position to object. After a few hours of intensive wheeling around and Young Ladying they tell me my leg's not broken, just badly bruised. It's really comically big now, like a Tom and Jerry cartoon. Just as well they cut my jeans off or I'd have had to limp home in knickers and bike boots, just to add embarrassment to injury. The elbow is cracked and I'm given a sling. Otherwise I'm just scuffed and dented but can go.

Back at the flat alone, I feel sore but impossibly elated; everything is vivid and sharp-edged, as if my eyes are focussing properly for the first time. It's almost uncomfortable and a bit frightening, but wonderful, excruciatingly wonderful. I sit and look at my hands, open and close them, turn them over and think how absolutely amazing they are, all those tiny bones and muscles, skin and nerves. I'm a bloody miracle, I am. I grab hold of this feeling and squeeze it tight, willing myself to never, never forget how this feels.

MY SISTER'S DAUGHTER

Lorraine H. Jenkins

THE IDEA WAS TO go along to my sister's scan, see the new baby ghost-like through her stomach and then head off to our favourite Italian restaurant and stuff ourselves on food we could never recreate. Nature decided against our plan though. The tired-looking doctor told us that my sister was four centimetres dilated and would have to stay put. I will admit that my first thought was those steaming hot meatballs that I would now be missing, but, excitement overtook hunger as I tried to remain calm in the face of my mother's rising panic.

'She hasn't got anything with her,' my mother protested as though that would somehow halt proceedings.

'It's OK, Mum,' I said, 'I'll go get her bag and things.' To be honest I was really glad to have something to do. A peck on the flustered cheek of my youngest sister and I was off. I don't think I released breath until I stood at the taxi rank outside the hospital. I can't remember much about the journey to mum's flat, the view from the window blurred into a high speed blend of muted colours. I just remember not wanting to be at that hospital at that point in time. I had only just had my own labour experience four months previously and wasn't sure that I wanted to see my sister go through that. I had been so relieved when she told me, shamefaced, that she wanted my mum to be her birth partner.

At the flat I managed to gather together the things a woman just can't live without in the hospital, I was about to lock the door on the way out when I received an anxious phone call from my mum. I held the phone to my ear as I locked the door, not really listening, just mum getting worked up.

'There's something wrong with the heartbeat,' she was saying.

'Whose heartbeat – Karen's?' I asked, not getting what she was telling me.

'The baby's,' her voice seemed foreign to me, she didn't sound like herself.

'What's wrong?'

I have since recognized that this is the point that a lifetime compressed itself into a day. I remember every millisecond of the journey back to that hospital, every mother and child waiting at traffic lights, every grey stone building that had seen better days, every half-naked Glaswegian man taking advantage of the slither of sunshine on that July afternoon. If I close my eyes I can even see the shoes on their feet.

When I got back, my mother's face was ashen, my sister was nowhere to be seen.

'They've taken her to the operating suite,' Mum said without meeting my eyes.

'What happened?' I let the heavy bag I was carrying fall at my feet.

'I don't know...they were monitoring her...that thing round her stomach, you know...and they couldn't find the heartbeat...so they did a scan and they just said the baby was in distress,' there was a look of wide-eyed distress on her face, of hopelessness, like she'd already accepted the most awful outcome.

'Is it serious?' I asked stupidly. I couldn't think of anything else to say. There was nothing I could do but swallow my fear and wait with my mum until they came and told us what was happening.

We waited for an eternity.

I could tell by the solemn look on the surgeon's face that it was not good news; '...not breathing...resuscitated...next 24 hours... abnormalities...distress...cord...'

That cold green hospital corridor seemed to stretch itself into infinity, I looked across at my mother who was nodding like she understood what was going on, the doctor put his hand gently on her shoulder and I saw her collapse. I've never seen a person implode before, but, that's what my mother did, right before my eyes the last piece of hope she was grasping at just floated away and she was left emptied. I couldn't open my mouth, how could this be happening? She was supposed to be having a run of the mill check up; this was supposed to be a day of joy.

'She's in the special baby unit, it's the best in the country, the best people...we'll monitor her closely,' he tried to reassure us. But, I could see in his eyes that it was pointless, the man must have had to go through scenes like this every day and he was trying to give hope where there was none.

'Thank you,' Mum grasped his hand and squeezed tightly. 'Can I see my daughter?'

'She's still groggy at the moment, but, you can sit with her, if you like.'

Ushered into the private room that is reserved for difficult cases we saw my sister weeping in her sleep. The nurse said the anaesthetic did that sometimes. I didn't believe her. My sister knew what had happened, she was awake but she didn't want to open her eyes to it.

We were eventually allowed to see Jadyn, my sister's daughter. She was tiny and surrounded by a mountain of machinery. They told us later that night that she was not going to survive. The strength my sister showed then is phenomenal to me, she arranged everything, family gathered to say 'hello' and 'goodbye' in the same breath, a priest baptised the baby, photographs that would have to last a lifetime were taken. I did nothing but look blankly into the camera and hold that child in my arms with no words sufficient to appease my grief or my guilt. I knew when I went home I would have a perfect baby girl to hold. I wanted that for my sister, the brave creature standing beside me telling me it was alright, it would all be alright, deserved her child to survive.

THE KING AND I

Gary Little

Hardeep Singh Kohli's favourite story

For most people the posters you had on your wall as a child would normally reflect the musical trends of the day, or the football team you supported. As a 13-year-old boy growing up in Glasgow this should have meant The Sex Pistols (if I was really cool) and Glasgow Rangers.

For my wall, I had a full size poster of Elvis Presley. I had bought the poster at the Barras for £2.50. This was his Vegas Years, electric blue jump suit, open from the waist up, with the heavy medallion finishing the look. I thought he looked amazing. On reflection, there was no reason why this overweight 41-year-old singer should have been in my life. It wasn't as if my parents were big fans. There were no LPs of his lying around, nor were there the blatantly lying anecdotal tales such as, 'Yir ma served Elvis a boatel a ginger when she worked at Prestwick Airport' to keep his name alive. I think most families in Glasgow had at least one member of their family that had a pop star story. 'Yer uncle Tam get aff wae that wee Lulu before she became famous'. At the time, it was just a cool looking poster.

There are many significant dates in modern history; Kennedy shot, Armstrong landing on the moon, the Berlin Wall collapse, and the planes crashing into the Twin Towers. These events will usually be followed by the question 'where were you when it happened?'. I can't answer for these events, but I can tell you where I was on 17 August 1977 when I heard Elvis Presley had died.

I was in the living room with my older sister watching *News at Ten*. The fact I was watching the news didn't show I had an interest in current affairs, but was a small sacrifice that allowed me to stay up late. As the news came to an end, Reginald Bosenquet, the newsreader that night, announced a newsflash 'we have just received a newsflash that Elvis Presley has died'.

My sister said 'that's terrible'. I said nothing. I got off my chair, walked up to my bedroom, shut the door and lay on my bed. I started crying. I had experienced crying before, I was a child, but this was a different feeling from the other times. On those occasions I had reason to cry, but why now? Why was I crying for this stranger? The simple fact I had never experienced the loss of anyone in my life before. No family deaths, not even the death of a pet to practise on. This was the first time, and it hurt.

WHEN DAD DIED

Morag MacInnes

WELL HE WAS ALWAYS an awkward rambunctious kinda bugger, an atheist in a town full of Wee Frees, a socialist in a county full of farming Liberals (they're worse than non-farming ones), the first Open University graduate in a world full of pulled-myself-up-by-my-bootstrappers. He died walking backwards, just to see if he could do it, having discovered that he could – again – walk frontwards, despite the hospital infections. Typical. Fell over and hit his head and died trying.

I saw him in the morning; I took the dog as usual into the old folks home. 'Aye aye,' said Vivian, 'thu'r here fur Ian.'

'Aye,' I said, 'me and Ivy.'

'Right, bonny dug,' says Vivian. 'Gie her a biscuit.'

'Hello, Mog!' he said. He never forgot my old family moniker, despite all the infarcts, the interventions, the short circuits, whatever you want to call the brain decay. He slurped the porridge, but it was still him, eating his porridge like he used to do at home with the clock ticking and my mum waiting for him to cook her scrambled eggs.

He was very happy. 'I did the test,' he said, 'I had to tie my laces. I tied them extremely well.'

The day before he'd had to have an assessment, to see if he was ready to come home. He had to describe how he would get up. He had to show how he'd dress himself. He had to describe where he'd be – the house he'd lived in and presided over for 40 years. He had to tell them who Tony Blair was. He did this without spitting, which was remarkable. I think he was being kind to the people from social services.

'I'll see you later, dear,' he said, 'because I'll be coming down the road home.'

'Yes you will Dad,' I said, 'and I've put mince on and a rhubarb crumble.'

'I like a crumble,' he said.

'I ken fine, Dad, that's why it's made. With milk, no custard.'

Then, because he was so happy, after I left, untied the dog and went home to get his bed ready and sort the mince – he got out of his chair, which pointed out towards the Flow and the sky, in the impossibly hot conservatory which old folks homes always have, to make the old folks feel connected to what they've left behind – and tried walking backwards, because he felt he was at last again in charge of his legs.

And fell over, you can guess it, and hit his head and didn't regain consciousness.

Vivian phoned. 'You might wanta come up,' she said.

So I spent the evening doing what you do, though you don't know that's what you do. I read him stories and told him things. He was curled up like a tired baby, breathing hard. I don't know if he heard them. In the end, Vivian came in and said, 'Have a cup of tea.' I took my eyes off him for one second, to say, 'Yes please, that's kind' and that's when the breathing stopped.

You can't imagine the dead face. But we put him in the studio where he painted all the pictures, and we all put stuff in his coffin beside him, books and drawings and flowers and lentils. That was another day, though, which also contained music and stories and poems and politically incorrect anecdotes. Squads of folk stretching down the street wanting to come to the celebration of his death. They had a fine time, he would have approved.

As for me, well, I won't forget him walking backwards after having his porridge; and expecting to get back home later for rhubarb crumble. It wisna the worst wey to go.

MY FATHER BROUGHT ME THERE WHEN
I WAS A CHILD

Andrew McCallum

Roddy Woomble's favourite story

BESIDE THE TRACK by the derelict station, where the railway leaves the cutting and shoots its arrow diagonally across the flat expanse of the Red Moss, the platelayers had built a brick bothy in which to shelter at piece-time. One of those platelayers was my grandfather; and sometimes on his 'spiv-days', when the weather was fair, my father would hoist me onto his shoulders and carry me through Station Wood to have my piece and some craic with the men.

'And whit have ye got in yer piece the day?' the Black Doc would ask, after I'd pushed my way through a turnstile of knees and squeezed into a crevice between the men who crammed the plank benches. The only light came from a doorless aperture let into the gable of the bothy's lee side, and the men were dark from their labour and the sun. I remember them mainly as redolent of stale sweat, damp clothing and tobacco.

I'd peep into the brown paper poke my gran had given me. 'Jam,' I'd tell him, trying to make my voice sound as deep and sonorous as the next man's.

'Damson or raspberry?'

I'd tear a bite from one of the sandwiches. 'Damson.'

'Uh-huh?' The Black Doc would weigh this information carefully. 'Hame-made or shop?'

'Hame-made!' I'd flare. 'Ma granny widnae hae shop-bought in the hoose!'

Then there'd be laughter, and the Black Doc would reach across the semi-darkness and buffet my head with his massive paw.

The Black Doc was a big man. The first time I saw him; I took him for a giant and kept the trunks of my father's legs between us. But after he'd finished his 'piece', drained the dregs of his tea from the bottom of his blackened billycan, and wiped his mouth and nose on the back of his hand, the Black Doc began to sing. He had a fine baritone voice, as rich and warm as polished walnut. Its vibration trembled in my stomach, and it wasn't long before I was being hoisted up onto his knee to 'oblige the company wi a sang'.

He must have been almost seven feet tall. He had to stoop to pass through the door; and even when he was sitting down, the bristle of his hair brushed the corrugated iron ceiling. And he was as broad as he was long, with shoulders like the boughs of the three massive beech trees that marked the northern extent of the village, and an immense blustery chest that filled the sails of his shirt. His forearms were the colour and texture of wood, beneath the hardness of which thick ropes of muscle and sinew snaked around hefty levers of bone.

But it was his feet that impressed me most. Shod in muckle calf-length boots, they were as long as my forearm and broad as railway sleepers. His boots were laced with blackened strips of hide, which criss-crossed their way up to the middle of his shins and looped the girth of his calves before being tied off in a small neat bow at the front. I was particularly struck by the neatness and precision of this lacing. Each chevron was the mirror-image of its counterpart. Each lay snug and straight against the leather tongue. Together they rose in perfectly parallel lines like the rungs of a ladder.

This day, my father tossed me onto his shoulders and tramped the path through Station Wood. As we rounded the bend that brought the crumbling platform into view, we saw my grandfather and his workmates gathered in a close knot by the side of the line.

I couldn't see the Black Doc. The men were conferring in low conspiratorial voices, their brows dark, their jaws grimly set. I wondered how their words could escape from behind such barely moving lips. Then one of the men spotted us and tugged at my grandfather's sleeve.

My grandfather glowered across at us, then detached himself from the group. My father slipped me from his shoulders and placed me carefully by the side of the path.

'You wait here a wee,' he murmured, laying a hand on my shoulder. 'Don't move. All right?'

He walked towards my grandfather and they exchanged a few words. Then my father turned on his heel and strode quickly back towards me.

The smile that had frozen on my face melted away like snow from a dyke. I looked from my father's face, to the face of my grandfather, to the faces of the other men. They were all watching me closely and their looks were overcast with a louring manhood secret into which I was about to be inducted.

A sudden gust of wind set the trees chattering and dust and debris from the path swirling into my eyes.

'The Black Doc!' I cried. 'Where's the Black Doc?'

Panic reared in my head, stomping its hooves and clapping its hands and bleating gleefully. A whirr of sparrows tore through the hedgerow, twittering excitedly in the bright summer sunlight. I ran towards the platelayers, angling my run to avoid the broadcast net of my father's arms.

'Wheesht, noo! Calm doon!' My father smothered me to his chest. His voice was warm and smooth and comforting. The men looked on, witnessing my passage, curious to see how well my father would facilitate it.

'The Black Doc's deid,' my father informed me. 'He was working by himsel on the line and a train struck him. He couldnae hae heard it comin.'

'How could he no have heard it?'

'I've nae idea.' My father shrugged. 'It happens. Onywise,' he went on, 'he's deid noo and that's an end o it. We'd better get ye hame.'

As we turned back along the path, I stole a glimpse down the track to the brick bothy. The Black Doc's feet protruded from the doorway, a hap of green tarpaulin skirting the top of his giant boots.

BE RESOLVED

Sara-Jane McGeachy

I MADE A NEW YEAR's resolution to try and eat breakfast every morning – set myself up properly for the day. On the first of January 2005 I woke up at 1.00 p.m. and had an Alka-Seltzer accompanied by a slice of cold pizza. It was all going to plan. On the second and third I managed something a little more nutritious. Then on the fourth of January I was due to return to work, so I got up and made myself five minutes late by having a bowl of Bran Flakes; very bad idea.

I put on my new boots and the trousers I had got for Christmas and headed out in to the wind and rain. I remember turning into Palmerston Place and feeling a little despondent that the holiday period was over. I'm not quite sure what made me look up, maybe it was instinct, or maybe I heard a noise, but something made me look to the top of the four stories of scaffolding towering above me. It was moving; slowly it seemed, tilting towards me. I began to run across the road – I think I was trying to out run the falling scaffolding, looking back that seems ridiculous, but in that instant it was all I could think to do. It turned out to be one of the best decisions I've ever made, a much better idea than the Bran Flakes. It's strange to think now that it was to be the last time I was able to run anywhere for the next two and a half years.

The noise was incredible, the sound of metal and masonry falling and hitting the ground. In the moment of silence that followed I realised I was pinned; face down to the wet pavement. I somehow screamed for help, hoping there would be someone to hear me. As the footsteps and voices came quickly towards me I became aware that the weight on my back was preventing me from breathing. I was suffocating and for the first time I was scared. The pain hadn't kicked in yet, I was able to say 'I can't breathe', drawing a tiny bit of air into the top of my lungs. I have often reflected that I would not have survived without the bravery and compassion of those strangers.

They were trying to lift off some scaffolding poles to alleviate the pressure on my body, but the ten-ton tangle of metal and wood was not going to shift easily. The disembodied voices were urgent but not panicked; a man was suggesting using a loose pole as a lever. Had anyone called the emergency services? Yes, someone had dialled 999. Then someone had a knife and cut the rucksack I was wearing from my back. They managed to raise the scaffolding a couple of inches and I somehow shifted out from underneath. I had become aware that my leg was broken.

Months later a cheerful surgeon told me: 'You're famous in the orthopaedic world!' as though he was informing me of a lottery win. Not only am I alive, but also able to walk and in possession of both legs after smashing my right femur with enough force to push the bone fragments through the front of my thigh, breaking six vertebrae in my spine and a still unknown number of ribs. Moving out from under the suffocating weight was tough.

A lady told me her name was Jo. Her voice was kind; she held my hand and told me I would soon be getting the care I needed. The nails on my fingers were chalk-white and saliva was dribbling from my mouth. A paramedic was kneeling on my other side explaining that the firemen were going to start freeing me, and then I could be given something for the pain. In hospital my dad would explain the sequence of events which followed and the importance of my sprint across the road would become apparent.

A streetlamp had snapped as it was hit by the falling scaffolding tower, it had bent, forming an arch which had prevented the full force of the metal hitting my body. Electric wires were protruding from the broken lamp and when the emergency services arrived on the scene there was a fear that the exposed wires would come into contact with the metal poles and the whole frame could go live. The process of freeing me could not begin until the electricity supply was cut.

Fear, confusion and a kind of desperation are the best descriptions I have for the thoughts in my head as I lay on a soaking Edinburgh pavement waiting for treatment. I was aware of the sparks emanating from the metal as the circular saws began their work. Apparently giant airbags were inflated to allow the medics in; they loaded me on to a stretcher and into the ambulance. I asked someone if I would be able to walk again; he asked if I could move my feet, and I could, I was able to feel my toes wiggling in my boots. At the hospital the new boots were cut from me, along with my new trousers, strange that I should even be aware of the loss.

The following days and weeks have taken on a disorientated,

nightmarish quality in my mind. I try not to reflect on it too deeply. But that day, setting out for work, started a new year which would be unlike any other before it and I pray, unlike anything I will ever experience again. I'm left now almost completely healed and thanking God (oh yes, I believe in Him now) for my life. Does it sound strange to say it was that day which taught me how good life can be, blessed with a family and friends who brought me through the darkest days of my life so far? I look forward with hope and the knowledge that a New Year's resolution is always made to be broken.

THE GOOD FIGHT

Gavin McNeill

A WEEK HAD passed since that fateful day, 28 December; a week in which the shock and horror of the terrible tragedy had not yet sunk in. The morning of the memorial service had arrived, the service to commemorate the life of one of the greatest people I have ever met, my friend Craig Macritchie.

All I could think about while putting on my suit that morning was how much he was looking forward to the prom, when he would be wearing a suit. The formality seemed strange; it was something I did not associate with Craig. Our relationship had always been informal. Somehow I had always thought my first time wearing a suit would be a proud moment, one in which I would be smiling and getting my picture taken. The reality could not have been more different.

I remember being dropped off at the train station, where I met up with my friends. The service would be held in town, and we decided to go in together, in the hope it would ease the pain a little. I think it did. At times like this, when one friend is lost, the others have to stick together and help each other through.

When we arrived we were astonished to find the vast number of people who had come to pay their respects. It really did highlight just what a guy Craig was, and how many lives he had managed to touch over so little time. The service itself was extremely painful. It really hit me that I was never going to hear his laugh anymore. I struggled to keep hold of my emotions while his cousins played a song which was written for the occasion by Craig's dad. Though this was overwhelmingly sad, at the same time it was comforting as it summed up how I was feeling at the time. It showed me how powerful music can be in capturing emotion. Everything I felt and wanted to say had been said in the song. It was almost as if the song was personal. From then on I was able to control my emotions better.

I did, however, realise that maybe my knowledge of Craig was less than I thought. It came out in the service that Craig attended church regularly, a fact that neither me, nor any of my friends were aware of. This saddened me terribly as I could not fathom his reasoning for keeping this part of his life completely private. Surely he didn't think we would have thought any less of him? That it would make him look less 'cool'? I just wanted to shout and tell him we didn't care about him going to church, that it didn't make a difference and he should have told us. I almost felt angry at him, then guilty because I knew I shouldn't.

There is one phrase which really stood out for me during the service. It was a quotation from the Bible, and I believed that it summed up Craig's life extremely well: 'I have fought the good fight. I have finished the race. I have kept the faith!' Craig was a fighter, he managed to hang on and battle away for four days before he was finally defeated.

Once the service had finished, we exited the church, each of us stopping to speak with Craig's devastated parents. This was by far the worst part of the whole day. What can you say to someone in that situation? I spoke with them a few moments, during which time a lump appeared in my throat. 'What a lovely service, I'm really sorry about Craig.' It hardly summed up how I felt about him, what a great person he was and how thankful I was to have known him.

My friends and I then decided to go for something to eat. All of us were unusually quiet, each absorbed in our own thoughts or memories of Craig. I remember thinking about the last time I had spoken to him. It had been the Friday before the accident, the last day of term at school, and we were walking up to church together. I couldn't remember what we were actually talking about. I just remember him laughing and joking, as he usually was. I just wish I could remember our actual conversation. At the time it seemed so unimportant, and that there would be many more to come.

We raised our glasses and proposed a toast to Craig. The collective sadness was overwhelming. As I remember, there were 15 of us at the table, and the staff had placed two tables for eight together, meaning there was one spare seat. I could not help but think that Craig should have been there, sitting round that table with us, amusing us all. As it was, neither a smile nor a laugh was to be seen or heard the entire time.

Nowadays, all I can think of is all that Craig has missed in the past few months; limbo dancing at the prefects' dinner, being in our limo at the prom; going through the excitement and anxiety of the exams and finally getting his results for those exams. All I have to remember though is that although his life was short, he still managed to achieve a lot. He fought the good fight. He finished the race. He kept the faith. And though it was hard at first, I now realise that death happens. It is inevitable, it just took this tragedy to make me understand.

CHRISTMAS EVE 1971

Liz McNeill Taylor

WITH FOUR SUBDUED children under 12 and a dog I drove from London to a village in the Scottish Borders, arriving at a half empty cottage as darkness was drawing in.

I drove with grim concentration, counting off the miles as they sped past, because I was running away from home. The thought of spending Christmas in my own house was beyond enduring. I had to get away from the telephone because it kept ringing and every time I answered it a concerned voice would say, 'I've just heard the most awful rumour. It can't be true, can it?'

The cottage to which I fled was cold and empty, furnished only with a few sticks of furniture left by the previous owners, but we soon had a log fire burning in the grate and spread our sleeping bags out on the floor in front of it. The children huddled around the hearth, wondering if they would be able to hang up their stockings. The baby, at two, was still young enough to believe in Santa Claus but the others were as stunned as I was and too tactful to bring up the subject.

In spite of the long drive, I was running on adrenalin-fuelled energy and went into the kitchen to prepare food, deciding for some reason to make custard to cover the slices of cold Christmas pudding I'd brought with me. The pudding had been made three months ago – before our world fell apart. I remembered sticking foil-wrapped sixpence pieces into the mixture and felt that the woman who did that had been a dewy-eyed innocent, somebody else, not me. As I stood stirring the custard my tears dropped into the pan and I watched them plopping onto its yellow surface like drops of rain.

My second daughter Sarah, who was ten, came into the scullery and put her arms round my hips. I hugged her and stopped crying because I knew I had to make some sort of an effort to give them a Christmas.

'It's warming up in there,' she said, 'It'll be fun sleeping on the floor – like camping.'

We'd never camped. We weren't that sort of a family. Their father preferred luxury hotels to campsites. But everything was different now. It had changed in ten minutes four weeks ago when he collapsed and died of a heart attack, most suitably in a world famous hotel in Singapore. He was 43 years old.

The thought of him, the memory of him, the smell of him, his very ghost was haunting us and it took a monumental effort not to burst out into communal wailing. It only needed one of us to start for the others to give way as well.

I'd brought brightly wrapped presents for the children with us in the car but even when they were piled by the fireside, they failed to cheer us up for the little room was bleak. There were no streamers, no balloons, no holly or mistletoe, no line of Christmas cards on the mantelpiece. Grateful for the leaping flames, we ate sitting on the floor while darkness filled the curtainless window. The garden that surrounded the cottage was silent except for the occasional hoot of an owl and the dog sat staring fixedly at the dark square of glass. She'd never heard an owl before. She'd rarely walked on grass in fact and when she did, she lifted her feet high as if she was afraid some hidden predator would bite her ankles.

The plates were gathered and piled in the sink and we were settling down to watch the flickering screen of an old black and white television when there was a knock at the front door.

The dog growled and we drew together, staring at each other. Who could be knocking? None of our friends knew where we were. We had never met anyone in the village. Should I answer the knock? I was still dithering when it was repeated, more sharply this time.

Guarded by the dog, I opened the door. A woman I had never seen before stood on the step with something bulky in her arms.

'Hello?' I said.

'You don't know me but I heard what has happened to you and one of the neighbours saw you arriving. I won't stay but I've brought you something,' she said, holding out the bundle.

It filled my arms and prickled my skin. It was a small Christmas tree, decorated with silvery tinsel and small brightly coloured glass balls. On the topmost branch the mysterious visitor from the darkness had stuck a star.

'Oh my God, you're an angel!' I said and started to cry.

She laughed, stepped into the hall and put her arms round me. 'I'm no angel. I'm just an old woman who likes children. Don't cry,' she said. 'You're going to be all right.'

All of a sudden I knew that what she said was true. We would be all right. We would survive the terrible thing that had happened to us. The unknown woman with the Christmas tree showed me that life goes on and that the kindness of strangers can help you through.

AN INCIDENT

Amy Rafferty

I'M WALKING THROUGH Partick, going over the bridge, heading to the shops.

I see a young man in front of me, straddling the bridge guard.

From where he's sitting it's about 50 feet down to a really shallow bit of the river, all rocks and moss, jagging out of the water.

I ask him if he's OK.

He has a fresh wound on his head that's needed stitches.

He tells me his wife left him for a junky, he can't see his kids.

It's his daughter's seventh birthday and this morning, he went round there to kill the junky.

He decided against it and instead, went to the hospital to get himself sectioned.

It didn't work so now he's here, straddling a bridge guard, about to jump into the river.

I ask him if he's taking the piss, he's grinning at me so it's hard to tell.

He shakes his head and spits down into the water.

I don't know what to say.

I ask him what his name is.

'Danny,' he says.

I ask him if his folks know he's here – he's texted them what he's about to do but hasn't told them where.

I start taking this more seriously than I was.

My mind is about to seize up and I'm wondering if the next thing I say is going to have him crashing down onto the rocks.

I look down into the water and tell him he'll not die if he falls, he'll break bones.

He tells me he's aiming his plunge onto the long, wide pipe that carries effluent over the river and really, that should do it.

Shaking my head I say, 'You really don't want to make a mess of yourself like that.'

We're both looking down now.

'How far d'ye think it is?' I'm asking.

'About 50 feet? Maybe?' says Danny.

About four years ago, one of my neighbours did this jump and he did die.

I don't tell Danny this. I tell him about the student who crippled herself trying the same thing, from the same spot. I'm wondering if my weird logic is going to help here.

He tells me to go on and enjoy the sunny day and I laugh, 'Aye, like that's a fucking option now.'

I phone the police.

Danny sits on the bridge guard and smokes. He drops one of his beers down into the water.

The police have been looking for him.

I come off the phone and ask Danny what his kids' names are.

He snorts, 'Did the polis tell you to keep me talking?'

I snort back, 'Naw, I just thought that up all by myself. I've seen this in the movies.'

We laugh again, shooting the weirdest breeze.

I tell him if he comes over to the right side of the bridge we can make plans to get this junky.

'We could tell the police about him. I'm sure the police'll do him in, they like doing stuff like that,' I say.

He asks me if I think he's a weirdo.

I shake my head, 'I think you're just sore.'

A policeman arrives. Danny starts shouting, telling him to piss off and then says sorry for being rude.

I take his apology as a good sign – if he was going to jump then he wouldn't care what either of us think about him.

The police close off the bridge and the fire brigade arrive with a big ladder and a wee boat and as the yellow incident cords go up and all the folk at each end go quiet, I'm struck that this is someone else's movie I've just walked into.

A doctor arrives.

He walks right up to Danny and puts his hand on his back.

It was all done in one wee movement and Danny looks safe again.

The policeman sidles up and whispers, 'Are you OK?'

I nod, eyes still fixed on Danny, he's looking at me while he talks to the doctor and I'm nodding my head with whatever the doctor says.

They'll not lock him up, no, they'll not put him in handcuffs, no, they will not.

Danny starts raving and screaming about this wee prick junky, how he was going to stab his face, how he's taken his family.

The policeman asks if I'm OK hearing this. I've already heard it so yes, I'm OK.

Danny shakes his head.

'I'm sorry, Amy, I didnae mean to drag you into all this,' he says.

'Don't be daft,' I tell him.

The policeman leads me away.

I shout over my shoulder, 'I'll speak to you soon Danny, OK?'

Danny starts screaming and banging his hands against the rail. I can't make out what he's saying and suddenly I'm scared.

He jumps up, over onto the RIGHT side of the bridge, back onto the pavement.

He's screaming and crying and I'm thinking he's done the bravest thing he could.

He stayed.

The police walk quietly towards him, two of them take his hands, not cuffing him, just holding his hands and another two come over and put their hands on his back.

It's weird to see him almost being cradled by these men, they are tender with him.

The crowd all started moving away, off into the park, some smiling and laughing, some shaking their heads. All of them turning to look at me, wondering what I was to do with this and I'm standing by the police cars wishing I had a cigarette.

A LITTLE BIT OF ME DIED THAT DAY, LITERALLY

Kevin Scott

DESPITE THE SIGNIFICANCE of the day I can never remember the date. I know it was in spring though. I always loved London in spring, although on this day I was due to have a malignant melanoma removed from my left ear.

6.45 a.m.

Mobile phone only survives being launched out the window as my freshly disturbed carcass is still trying to come to terms with the tuneless shrill emanating from its bastard alarm.

7.05 a.m.

I'm out the door wincing as the sleep in my eye dislodges itself in the wind.

7.25 a.m.

Arrive at Charing Cross hospital in Fulham and find Ward 11 with an ease that belies my semi-conscious state. Armed with a freshly purchased newspaper I open the ward doors and cross the threshold. Immediately ponder why I've not taken advantage of my £40 a month private health care.

7.30 a.m.

Shown to my bed. Initial thoughts that I am in the morgue are soon dispersed by my neighbour's snoring. Despite my lethargy, I don't feel right about getting into bed, so plump for the chair.

7.45 a.m.

Tests done. Discover I weigh 14 stone. How?

8.30 a.m.

Drink the worst cup of coffee of my life.

9.00 a.m.

A package arrives! 'A pair of anti-embolism thigh high stockings'. Told I must don them, along with a gown, at noon. Surely it wasn't like this in *M*A*S*H**?

9.10 a.m.

Three doctors come to stare at my ear. Told I'm 'in for a long wait'. Once again I think about the empty private room with TV and air-con.

11.01 a.m.

Depressed by my groaning comrades and with fingers blackened by reading every inch of the paper, I decide to venture into the TV room.

11.05 a.m.

Return to bed/chair area. Morning TV is rubbish. Note that NHS may be on its knees but it can still put Pip Schofield's coupon on a 28 inch widescreen TV.

11.10 a.m.

Eastern European boy on the ward who bears a staggering resemblance to what I think Burt Reynolds will look like in 2015 chats to me about the hassle he's been having getting released, as his pills aren't ready. Poor Burt.

11.25 a.m.

Order lunch. Veg pâté and an apple. Yum.

11.30 a.m.

Anaesthetist arrives. Informs me I can't eat lunch. Raging. I'm already starving.

11.40 a.m.

Burt Reynolds is leaving. He dashes past with his bag and waves as he rants at a nurse. Give 'em hell, Burt. His wife smiles at me. She looks nothing like Burt's ex-wife Lonnie Anderson.

12.01 p.m.

I defy the gown and stockings deadline. Realise my masculinity is living on borrowed time.

12.15 p.m.

Lunch arrives. Am suddenly thankful I can't eat it, but can't help but wonder why they brought it?

12.25 p.m.

Nurse Gina tells me to change. I've been dreading this.
Points picked up during changing: tying knots behind one's back is murder; as is putting on stockings.

12.30 p.m.

Walk past a mirror and am frozen by some unknown force; possibly fear, possibly abject humiliation, possibly arousal.

12.40 p.m.

The hunger is intense. Contemplate stealing next door's yogurt. He's in bed looking rough as hell. What's he going to do?

12.58 p.m.

Lack of food, sleep and stimulating conversation is taking its toll on my cross-dressed body. I wish Burt were still here.

1.34 p.m.

Some boy arrives and orders me into bed. I've got rather attached to my chair but I suppose needs must. I hop on and the brakes are taken off. We're away.

TIME UNKNOWN

I'm in the theatre looking like an extra from ER. I check out the operating slab from my port-a-bed and wonder how many people have died on it. Decide to work on the presumption I won't be the next. Doc arrives and gives me three jags. It's utter agony. Not the jags you understand, but the doc's informal banter.

My eyes are covered. I never even got a chance to say goodbye. I wanted to see. Saying that, it sounded horrible. Snip, snip; bye bye ear lobe.

TIME UNKNOWN

We're done and I'm being wheeled into the 'recovery room'. Laugh at the irony, as I've felt worse after two lunchtime Stellas.

Various tests done. I watch my heart rate and see how low I can get it. It drops to 64; calm as a Hindu cow.

2.35 p.m.

Back on the ward and it's time to become a man again. Haven't ripped tights off so fast since the time I pulled that Sonia look-a-like. I pull off my heart monitor pads, which hurts more than the ear thing did. Check out the remainder of my ear and reckon it'll make a good 'I was saving a puppy when' story.

2.36 p.m.

Jacket on, and I'm out the door waving at the nurses as I pass them. Unfortunately I'm ordered back to my chair, as I need to see a doctor and eat something before I can be discharged.

2.48 p.m.

One cup of rank coffee and two bits of toast later and I'm itching to head. Where's the doctor?

3.10 p.m.

Bored. Take walkman out my bag and prepare to rock. As I lower the headphones over my ears I quickly realise the joke's on me.

Circa 4.00 p.m.

Nurses are meant to be kind. Why would she tell me the doctor won't be here till half five then?

4.00–5.00 p.m.

'The snooker years'. Am depressed further in the TV room by Peter Ebdon's negativity on the baize. The afternoon brightens up some-what though, when I notice someone has scrawled 'fatty fatty fatty' on a picture of Lisa Riley in OK magazine.

5.08 p.m.

Tea time. Beef Cobbler and potato wedges.
Three bites in I decide I'm on hunger strike. 'Free the Fulham One!'

5.54 p.m.

Three doctors turn up and take a nano-second to decide I can go home. Probably saw the potential law-suit from my hunger strike and played the diplomatic card.

5.55 p.m.

I'm waiting on the lift.

5.56 p.m.

I'm going down.

5.57 p.m.

I'm outside in the rain.
I love London in spring.

THE DAY WAR BROKE OUT

T. Henry Shanks

IT WAS SEPTEMBER and another hot Sunday morning.

As the Commanding Officer of a British Tank Division I was leading an invasion through enemy territory. But my dinky toy tank was making slow progress along the soft cushion of catmint in the herbaceous border beside the open scullery door.

Then I heard the announcement we had all been waiting for. The voice seemed thin and reedy. Maybe it was the overheating of the valves again inside my father's homemade wireless set.

The words 'war' and 'Germany' were clear enough. And something about 'undertaking'. I knew that was something to do with arranging burials. I remembered my grandfather's funeral. Things were serious.

Around the corner of the back door I could see my mother and father sitting in their usual places at the kitchen table – opposite each other – but unusually they were holding hands across the pale blue oilcloth cover.

I jumped up and ran down the garden path to the shed where my brothers were busy building a balsa wood model of a Spitfire. I could not help screaming with excitement…'We're at war with Germany! It's on the wireless.' They both breinged out of the hut and we all ran back to the house. Leaping and shouting, 'It's war! It's war!'

We dodged round our father's prize strawberry bed which had already been earmarked for an air raid shelter and skirted the rhubarb patch, soon to be a hen run as part of the War Effort. But that was all the future…

My imaginings were brought to a halt when I saw my mother standing at the back door waiting for us. Her arms were folded across her apron as usual. I thought that I was to get a row for screaming in the garden. But she wiped her cheeks which were wet and said very quietly, 'You heard then. Well, I hope it won't be as long as the last one.' She held each of us by the shoulders for a minute and looked into our faces. She wasn't one for crying much but I could see that she was upset. Our father came up behind her and put his arms around her. We had not seen him do that before. He said to us gruffly, 'On you go now. Out and play...while you can.' We hurried off down the lane, our bare feet hardly touching the hot cobbles.

The important thing was that we could now play a new 'Gang Game' – the British Army against the Germans. Better than our usual games of cowboys and Indians or cops and robbers which were getting a bit stale. Not only that... This was real.

I began thinking out the plot...

We needed some bigger boys on our (British) side. Most of us could manage some sort of uniform. Our Boy Scout belts would help and we all had balaclavas. The neckerchiefs were no use. They were only used for cowboys...the girls could stay as nurses for the wounded. They had already had major parts in our game of nurses and doctors. Our mothers did not approve of that game anyway and it had always to be acted out in the draughty Big Pend – away from parental eyes. Some of us had already been issued with gas masks but we knew that they weren't supposed to be for playing with. They would stay in their cardboard boxes unless taken out for official practices at school. We could always camouflage our faces. I had a paint box.

Suddenly my boyish imaginings came to an abrupt halt as some loud jarring notes surged from the newly constructed siren on top of the police station. It became a loud wail which blasted over the grey bulk of the hosiery factory and around the tall chimney of the skinworks. Until the noise enveloped the whole town.

It was my first experience of an air raid warning. Suddenly I was no longer just an eight-year-old boy. I came to attention as I had been taught at my Tuesday night Cub meetings.

Eventually the noise moaned into a long silence. Then I heard the clanging of the ancient church bells in the town steeple. It was a familiar sound and I relaxed. I actually stood at ease. It was to be six years before I was to hear that familiar sound again.

Sports and Travel

THE ILLICIT STILL

Paula Douglas

IT WAS THE LATE 1970s and we'd been living in Libya for five years. Dad was a teacher who successfully supplemented his meagre salary by running an illicit still. He wasn't the only moonshiner in town, but it was widely acknowledged among Tripoli's expatriate community that he was the best. He'd bought the still off an old oilman not long after we first arrived and smuggled it into our villa one night, under cover of darkness, having first tried to disguise it by dressing it up in one of my old nighties and sellotaping a doll's head to the top of it. To Mum's disgust, the grotesque doll-still was then installed in her and Dad's ensuite bathroom. Shortly after-wards, he moved several large black plastic dustbins into the out-houses above the garage and began filling them with the raw mash from which he would eventually make his own peculiarly potent brand of liquor. The mash was a deceptively simple-sounding base of sugar, water and yeast; the trick was to get the proportions right. For months the bins spewed out a frothing, noxious ooze as Dad struggled with the formula. He scuttled about like some mad scientist, anxiously checking the contents of the bins, running batch after batch of mash through the hissing, bubbling still until, one day, he staggered exhausted but triumphant from the bathroom.

'I've done it!' he announced.

My younger sister Emma and I peered at the bottle in his hand. The liquid inside looked just like water. We were unimpressed. 'But what does it do, Dad?'

'It makes your old man rich, girls, that's what it does!'

It never made him rich, but for a few years it was, as they say, a nice little earner. By 1978, his hooch had assumed a reputation of near-legendary proportions and he'd scaled up operations significantly to cope with surging demand. The black bins multiplied, the still never stopped and we were the only family in the neighbourhood whose sugar consumption was 100 kilos a month, and rising.

Alcohol was banned in Libya and, although the authorities often turned a blind eye to the thriving booze black-market, police raids were still a regular occurrence. Having no desire to see the inside of one of Libya's notorious prisons, Dad had tried to be discreet about his activities, but his enterprise was one of the worst-kept secrets in Tripoli. The stream of late-night visitors and the ever-present sweet reek of fermenting mash which hung about our house were dead giveaways. But the boot to the door never came and, like the bogeyman you stop believing in, Dad's fear of arrest gradually diminished. Convinced that the police had somehow forgotten about him, he started to relax, cranking up production even further. He should have known better; they were simply biding their time.

All of this was the backdrop to what was, for my sister and me, an idyllic life. While our parents and their friends dreamed of the day they could finally pack up and leave Libya for good, we couldn't imagine living anywhere else. We loved our carefree, barefoot existence and, after five years, we were still in thrall to the sheer exoticism of the place, to the sights, sounds, smells and tastes whose very strangeness had become familiar and comforting.

28 March 1978: the day I turned 12. In the early afternoon, Emma and I headed to a friend's house to watch an imported video, a birthday treat since, for most expat families, a television set was a rare luxury. We were halfway through our second episode of *Starsky and Hutch* when a friend of Mum and Dad's arrived. Betty was tear-stained and shifty, beckoning aside the owner of the house, talking in the urgent undertone used by all bearers of bad news, while all the time shooting furtive glances in our direction. We didn't need to be told what was going on; we knew instantly what had happened; and, in one of the few moments of clarity during what was to become an almost dream-like blurring of days, I understood that something had shifted irrevocably, that the life we had known and loved was over.

We found out later that the police had raided the house that afternoon, as Mum and Dad were drinking coffee and eating slices of my birthday cake with friends. They arrived mob-handed, led by the local chief of station, a dubious honour and one that didn't bode well for a happy outcome. The house had been ruthlessly turned over and Dad had watched in agony as barrel after barrel of his precious mash was poured into the bath and disappeared down the plug-hole. The still was taken away, although Dad was reunited with it a few days later when, in a bizarre piece of public service programming, he was paraded on Libyan television and asked to give a demonstration of how to make moonshine.

Over the next week, my sister and I were ferried around between different friends' houses before being flown back to the UK in the company of two burly oil workers. We didn't see Mum or Dad again for three months. Dad spent most of those in jail. He eventually skipped the country on a fake passport while out on bail and pitched up on my grandparents' doorstep in Dalgety Bay in late June. Mum followed a week later, having spent her remaining days in Tripoli in hiding, hardly daring to breathe until her Alitalia flight had crossed the coastline out into the Mediterranean en route to Italy.

We never saw Libya again.

32 BOXES

Trish Elms

'RICK JAMES IS COMING with us and so is Abba,' I declare. My husband is rolling his eyes, silently drawing the line at the soundtrack to *Xanadu*.

As per usual, with all the good intentions in the world, we've left everything to the last minute. Now, with only a day to go, we're faced with the monumental task of sorting lives accumulated over the space of five years in Canada into 32 small brown cardboard boxes to be transported across the continents to start anew in Scotland. Well, with a bit of luck, anyway.

Have we lost our minds? Conceivably, yes. If we were more sensible or organised, we would have developed a plan, or at the very least neat little lists in which to logically compartmentalise our belongings in order of importance. But who am I kidding – that would have been far too sane and probably more difficult in the long run. How do you choose Pulp over REM? It's impossible and so we'll take both.

Scotland isn't completely foreign to me. I lived there once before with little more than the contents of the rucksack on my back. Back then who needed more than a few cherished CDs, a decent fitting pair of jeans, a few clean pairs of underwear (you just never know when you'll get lucky or wind up in hospital) and a journal to scribble the intimate details, immortalising the adventure? But that was nearly a decade ago, I was younger, more adventurous and adaptable then, and had far less stuff. I was possibly also slightly more foolish and certainly far less materialistic.

Now starting a life with less than everything I began with seems daunting.

Thankfully we don't have the hassle of trying to transport an entire flat's worth of possessions across the ocean. We've sold most of our furniture, really everything and the kitchen sink, to the girl who will shortly take up residence in the tiny apartment that has been our home for the past five years. We have left pieces of our lives hidden in these wooden floorboards, mastered the art of making a mostly edible dinner in a claustrophobic kitchen, and shared secrets between the sheets of a well-used bed. If walls could talk, this new tenant would hear many tales of laughter, sorrow, love and friendship.

Maybe like me, she thought the summer of 2005 seemed as good as anytime to change a life. She beamed enthusiasm and in ways reminded me of myself, full of optimism; compelled by the beginning of a new chapter in her life and the prospect of having a place to finally call her very own. I hope she will enjoy it here, and remember to water the plants now and again. They now also belong to her.

But there remains the business of selecting the finalists and ultimate winners that will begin this new Scottish existence with us across the sea. Beyond the obvious books, shoes, clothes, photographs and sentimental trinkets, it's difficult to know what will stay and what will go. When staring you in the face, it's nearly impossible to decide what you could actually live without.

I hardly know where to begin, and so we inadvertently start with Rick James and the vast music collection that two people have acquired over the span of a lifetime without and with one another. As I face the towering pile of CDs and vinyl, I realise that this has little to do with logic and is more about heart.

Sifting through the pile of music I discover that not all Rick's are equal; letting go of quick-and-easy musical guff is painless, surprisingly freeing; kind of like disinfecting the soul. I feel strangely liberated as I place the offending CDs in the shoebox marked 'Darren', a friend with a music collection so abysmal that our offerings of Ace of Base and Rick Astley will actually make a small improvement.

What benefit can be found in keeping two copies of CDs that will only take up precious space in our 32 boxes? And yet, neither of as are willing to part with our respective cherished copies of OK Computer or the Counting Crows' ethereal August and Everything After. Same CDs, different memories, different countries, different lifetimes. Carefree student days when we longed for nothing more than long lie-ins and late nights with cheap beer. I didn't know him then and I don't drink beer anymore, but the memories that come flooding back can't be as easily discarded and so the duplicates will travel in box 22 together.

We spend the afternoon shuffling through our lives, finding

well-loved books, faded love letters and reviving nearly forgotten moments in photographs. By dinner time, box after box is filled until a mountainous brown wall emerges in our hallway with 'this way up', 'fragile' and 'handle with care' printed across it in his erratic handwriting. 'Careful, this is the remains of our lives, handle with the utmost respect, care and concern or suffer the wrath of lady karma' would have been more appropriate, but far too long.

They'll be picked up and shipped off tomorrow, as will we, boarding a plane for the west of Scotland and the new life that awaits us there.

Physically our apartment doesn't appear that different. Same deep blue musty coach, wooden coffee table on wheels and large abstract Ikea print remain, serving as reminders that we were here. And yet, everything has changed. A new life has begun; our past life entrusted to the hands of the shippers.

Along with our other carefully chosen belongings, I'm hopeful that in roughly a month's time Rick (James), Olivia Newton John, Bjorn, Benny and crew will meet us in Glasgow, ready to set the soundtrack for the new life we are about to build.

BOTTLE

Robbie Handy

AH TOOK THE BOTTLE o beer wi ma left hand an opened the fridge wi ma right. Ah put it on the top shelf, between the cheese an butter, like a wee shrine. Ah breathed deep: 'that'll taste good the night', an padded out the kitchen tae get ready for war.

Kitbag: bandages, shorts, boots, gumshield, vest. Ah looked at the vest, it sez DUNFERMLINE ABC. Ah ran the bath hot an deep. The water eased ma bones an ah sooked the steam in slow. Ah prayed; 'Dear God, protect me an ma opponent'. Then ah stood up an shook the water off like a big rabid dug. Let's go!

Ah walked past the street an winked at the sign sez; ROBERT WILSON COURT. Past Toonhill school an up tae the top o Toonhill Road. Waited at Robby Road for ma lift. Phone rings an ma Dad sez 'Mind duck this time, son'. Van crunches on the corner an coach Tommy sez 'jump in big yin, we're late'.

Through tae Falkirk an ah jumped out an stretched ma arms in the fog. The sign sez: HMP POLMONT. Turnkey took us through tae the changin room. Ah was superheavyweight, an ah knew who ma boy wis straight off, the biggest one there, a boy fae Alloa. Ah'd sat wi ma demons all night when Mike, ma second, comes in: 'Two minutes mate, ye warm?' – 'Aye,' ah'd shadowboxed for 10 minutes an had a slick sheen o sweat on ma body. Ah stood up wi ma wee razor gloves an walked through. The crowd wis high an rumbled, 'Ohh, here we go,' as ah passed, like impending doom. Mike geen me a wee drink an Tommy sez 'this'll be hard mind' as ah turned an the bell dinged.

Ma southpaw right flicked at his face, an ah wis relived tae be finally leatherin him. Ah like tae draw first blood, so ah hit him wi a left cross, then got caught wi an uppercut as he tried to bull me wi his size. Ah knew ah shouldnae mix it, cos the round wis half up an ah wis knackered.

Puggled an gaspin, ah got caught wi three or four big, boomin punches. Ah stepped out o range, an ah'm ashmed tae say, but ah had a wee moment o doubt: 'What am ah doin here, ah'm too old for this'. But what could ah do? Gie up an walk out the ring? no chance, when ye get in, there's only two ways out, on yer feet at the last bell, or on a stretcher. So ah gritted ma teeth an rushed head-long intae hell. Ah caught an uppercut wi ma palm under ma chin, tied him up an bulled him intae the corner. Then ah melted him wi a big left hook as the bell dinged again.

In the corner, Tommy laughed: 'Huv ye anythin left?' as he sponged ma face an ma blood ran down ma chest in wee red rivers. He sez, 'Huv a blaw in this round.'

For once, ah followed orders an stayed outside. The boy kept goadin 'come on, son' an wavin me in wi his gloves. After ah smacked him a few times, he shut his mouth. Ah went cornerward well rested. Tommy sez, 'That's better. Robbie, now ye can chin him.' As ah went out for the last round, raw power bunched in ma hands an ma veins flowed fire. Ah slashed him wi left hooks an uppercuts an even wi his height, ma jab found home. Dinnae get me wrong, he caught me wi some gid yins, specially a straight right that shook me fae ma chin, down ma spine tae the soles o ma boots. He didnae like ma power though, and started runnin. He'd gone fae bull tae matador. Then ah jabbed and winged intae him wi a wide left hook an caught him flush. Ah knew, cos ah'd aimed six inches through his head for power, an ma hand went through his face. He rocked an stumbled, but gie him dues, stayed upright. The final bell rang an the crowd roared up. Ah didnae win, but lost a close decision. Ah patted the boy's shoulder an sez, 'Good fight, mate.'

When ah stepped out the ring, a brunette lassie flashed a smile: 'Well done, doll' she winked. Ma face wis numb an ah tasted gunmetal blood. Ye see, for us fighters, the broken noses, closed eyes, cracked teeth an sliced lips are the canvas of our bloody art. It's beautiful an visceral, an if ye didnae like it, ye wouldnae buy it. When ah got ma glove off, Tommy shook ma hand an back in the changin room, he sez tae the wee ones, 'Dae ye see this boy? That's courage.'

We left the jail, home tae Fife. Ah crunched up ma steps, shut the door an took off ma T-shirt. Ma left shoulder wis burnin fae the hooks. Ah said a wee prayer tae thank God for protection. Ah opened the fridge door wi ma right hand an took out the bottle o beer wi ma left. Ah bit off the top wi ma teeth an took a long, cool draught. It tasted good.

ARABIAN NIGHT

Louise Laurie

IT'S JUST PAST midnight in downtown Jeddah and the locals are out to play. It's pitch black, hot and humid. The streetlights are ablaze and there's the usual cacophony of car horns. Lolling in the back seat of a brown Buick, I survey the scene. The Oak Ridge Boys are blasting 'Elvira' from the CD player and I feel like dancing.

I assume there's a pretty good chance I may be dancing soon. I'm on my way to a wedding reception. Yes, I know it's the wee small hours – but I'm on my way to a wedding reception, no kidding. Samir (my Arabic friend) has allowed Catherine (his new American wife) and myself to be guests at the reception at some swanky five star hotel. Neither Catherine nor myself know the bride and groom nor what to expect when we arrive at The Sheraton. Samir chooses not to enlighten us. We are mere women, after all...He, meantime, for some obscure reason is dressed in chocolate-coloured corduroy trousers and a green checked shirt. I think idly to myself that he wouldn't look out of place felling trees in deepest Canada.

We arrive. All swishing silk, shimmering hair and made-up faces. Catherine's in powder blue from head to foot and I'm swaddled in boring old beige but I had no choice (the dress was a gift from Samir, reassuring himself that no cultural faux pas would occur while he was in charge). We're two floors up and the banqueting suite is the size of two football pitches, twinkling with an obscene amount of intricate chandeliers. Many well-dressed, exotic Arabic women have also made their entrance. The noisy chatter and the mingling, heady perfumes assail my senses. I think it's just as well this is a 'dry' country and no alcohol is allowed. I'm getting drunk on the atmosphere alone.

As I follow Catherine towards elaborate chairs arranged in neat rows, I think – Saltcoats to Saudi Arabia is one heck of a culture shock. More 'shocks' soon follow. There will be no men present, there will be no children allowed, there will be no music...

We stand out like sore thumbs. We are the only two Westerners there. The language barrier necessitates a lot of smiling. They all smile at us. We smile back. I didn't realize till then that your face can become quite sore through prolonged smiling. We continue to sit and smile at our fellow female guests. Someone is passing round huge platters of party food. It's all sweet, very sweet. Little almond cakes drenched in honey, pistachio nuts and a mountain of dates. I take a token morsel. I'm so punch drunk with the whole scenario that I don't know if I'm thirsty or hungry.

Suddenly there's an almighty racket at the front seats. Has someone taken ill? Has someone fainted in the heat of all these bodies? Nope. It's music, Jeddah style. The women are clicking their tongues and making music. To my ears, it sounds like Indian squaws round the campfire. It's senses overload by now and I sit quietly and try to take it all in. I wish I had a camera but, yep, you've guessed it – they're not allowed. This 'music' is because the bride and groom have suddenly appeared – from nowhere it seems. I certainly didn't see them arriving. I feel as if I'm outside of my body looking in. I try to concentrate on the proceedings. I'm well aware that this is a one-off and that I may well be trying to remember every precious minute for many years to come. The happy couple are ensconced on ornate gold thrones (and we all thought Posh and Becks were the first, eh?) to receive their guests. I watch. I join the queue of well-wishers which is long and snakes round the room. At last I am 'received' graciously and in silence. I proffer a small gift. They smile their thanks. When the last of the guests have been received, the groom disappears and the dancing and making-merry commences.

Small huddles of women dance. This is a rare event for extended families to mix and mingle, gossip and chat, preen and prance. To strut their stuff without the restrictions of their menfolk. Having lived in the country for five years, I am painfully aware that this 'freedom' is as delicate and as fragile as a butterfly.

Protocol dictates that Catherine and myself sit demurely. We sit demurely. The 'music' continues to rain down on us over the next six hours or so. What with the brittle-bright artificial lighting and the unusual sounds all around, I find the whole event surreal.

Dawn breaks and it's the cue for the end of the party. We're all pretty tired by now. The 'music' has petered out and the food and soft drinks have been devoured. Time to call it a night – literally. Samir, our driver and escort appears at the hotel entrance as if by magic. He drops me off at our compound near the Red Sea coast. I thank him profusely and realize that I'm dog-tired. Common sense suggests that I roll into bed and sleep. It's been a long day's night, after all. But I don't want to sleep. I can't sleep. I'm too tired to sleep. The phrase 'I'll sleep when I'm dead' pops into my head. My husband has already left for work. I glance at the kitchen clock. It's 7.15 a.m. I want to share my experience with someone... anyone. My head is bursting with a zillion thoughts. I have a quick shower and change, ready for work at the British Embassy.

As far as I'm aware, no current British expatriate has been a guest at an Arabic wedding reception...until now.

THE ACHNASHEEN DESOLATION

Murdo Macleod

Evelyn Glennie's favourite story

There was a time in this fair land when the railroad did not run.
When the wild majestic mountains stood alone against the sun.
Long before the white man and long before the wheel.
When the green dark forest was too silent to be real.

THESE ARE THE OPENING LINES of Gordon Lightfoot's Canadian Railroad Trilogy, a song nobody remembers but which takes me straight to my day like this.

It was late August 1982, one Monday morning, when I clambered into the old cycling gear – thick tartan shirt, v-neck sweater, brown corduroys and worn trainers – and mounted my five-speed Raleigh to embark on the opening day of an epic journey from Inverness to the Isle of Harris, stopping at Torridon and Broadford. There were four of us – my twin brother John, my cousin and friend Norman and our school friend Andrew.

Leaving Inverness, we snaked along the shore of the Moray Firth to Beauly, through Muir of Ord, into the enormous wilderness landing in Achnasheen. Those few words convey nothing of the agony of that unspeakable 43-mile tragi-comic struggle against the forces of nature and unsuitably tight trousers. Our cycling styles matched our personalities – Norman out in front, taking the wind without compromise, strong and persistent, and unnecessarily serious; John, apparently carefree and optimistic, prone to bizarre mechanical failures; Andrew, inexperienced but determined to enjoy himself, progressively worn out by sprinting and resting repeatedly; and me, tucked in, talking and singing incessantly, wanting only to be heard and not seen.

By lunch we were spent. A gusting, obnoxious head wind had driven the life and spirit out of us as we wobbled, jelly-legged, into the pub at Achnasheen. John bought a round to refresh us, and in a moment, Andrew drained his pint. Soon after, we found him, with an unsettlingly beatific expression, leaning back holding the roller towel in the bathroom. Andrew was, like me, unimpressively twiglike, but even his weight was too much for the towel, which split with a satisfying zing, depositing Andrew on the tiled floor. I have no idea what Andrew was feeling – he said nothing throughout – but it improved our morale no end.

We started out again, stiff and bloated from too many chips. An elderly American stopped us to engage in conversation. Maybe he just felt we looked like we needed encouragement. When we rode off, he called after us, 'OK, lads, heads down – butts up!'

Some may call Achnasheen the jewel of the Highlands; it may have produced men and women of renown and beauty; but that day it felt like the heel of Andy Murray's sock. Glad we were to shake the mud of the place from our Golas.

Twenty minutes out, a driver waved us down. 'Boys, you left your coat at the pub!' Not ours, we confirmed. A shrug and he continued on his way. Who knows whose coat it was? By this point, we were becoming mildly hysterical.

As we slowly ascended out of the village it dawned on us that the road sharply inclining away from us was the only road to the west, and that's where we would have to go to reach a bed for the night.

The hill, leading to a crest with a justly admired view of Loch Maree and Kinlochewe at its foot, was a slow, desperate climb, with no apparent respite, exposed its full length to the whipping wind which obviously didn't much fancy us. Norman summarised the situation through half-closed eyes, John Wayne about to lead the herd in Red River, and got on with doing what he did best – leaving us behind. I followed at a slightly forlorn distance, with John cajoling Andrew to get it in first and take his time.

I thought we were doing pretty well. Hill climbing is, crucially, about rhythm. Get into a pattern of breathing, pedalling and pulling, and the unbearable pain recedes into barely manageable torment. Never stop. Let me make that clear. When you're on a long climb, never stop. It's a nightmare getting started again so nobody ever stops. It's an unspoken bond among us not to stop.

Andrew stopped. John called us back. I turned to see, fatally lost momentum, and gave in, turning to wheel back to the layby where Andrew had reached his limit. Norman eventually realised what had happened, and returned, seething.

Andrew, who by this stage was sitting on a rock gazing over

the valley with an enigmatic face, spoke indistinctly. John, torn between sympathy and an unstoppable urge to burst out laughing, translated. He said, 'Leave me alone, boys, I want to die'. There was a pause. In the silence, breached only by the howling of what I believed was the wind but could have been Norman, I saw that Andrew hadn't just dismounted. He had tossed his bike aside with disdain. You can't do that. It's your steed, your boon companion, your only way to get to dinner that night.

John mediated with Andrew and eventually persuaded him to return to his vehicle. I did nothing, but very effectively, as Norman didn't kill Andrew, but turned and resumed his climbing.

The rest of that ride remains with me, a vivid waking nightmare. When we reached Torridon we had been utterly wiped out by the head wind, and having misjudged the distance had suffered the grave disappointment of shelter being 10 miles further than we had thought. We barely spoke that evening. We were too tired to argue, and too demoralised.

You might think that arriving would be glorious relief, a chance to stop and rest, warm up, dry out and restore the juices with a good meal. We got all of that, but only one thought preoccupied us that night.

It's going to be just as bad tomorrow.

BROKEBIKE MOUNTAIN

Chris McCahill

WE'D BEEN TOLD that 'it's the kinda road where you can watch your dog running away for a week'; the kind of road that art tutors draw when teaching perspective to demonstrate how parallel lines converge at a vanishing point on the horizon. Route 22 runs north across Canada's Kananaskis region (where *Brokeback Mountain* was filmed) and is your original 'lonesome highway'. Having read Jack London as a kid I'd always wanted to hear *The Call of the Wild*. Little did I know how wild it would be.

The day dawned ominously. The news warned that there would be no let up in the wettest June in Canadian history and the blackening sky suggested that the arrival of the four horsemen of the Apocalypse was imminent. The last road sign as we pedalled out of town was equally foreboding: 'Warning – No services for the next 128 km'. Then there was the curse of the cycle tourist – the headwind.

With a tailwind you feel unstoppable. 'Oot the way, Lance Armstrong and Chris Hoy! I'm carrying panniers, a tent and loads of other junk that I should never have brought but I'll take the lot of you!' It's glorious.

With a headwind in such BIG country you don't feel quite so smug. The only time Mark Beaumont looked like he might abandon his record-breaking round-the-world cycle was after days in a headwind on the Nullarbor plain in Australia. It tests the resilience of even those with record-breaking determination. The brain isn't convinced you're moving and that 'vanishing point' remains just over the horizon, always just out of sight.

But what the hell! We'd already survived worse; mountain blizzards and stinging hailstones, snakes and man-eating spiders. We had dodged tumbleweeds in the Arizona desert and evaded whoopin', hollerin', pick-up drivin' red-necks trying to run us off the road in Wyoming. We had even frightened off a grizzly in Yellowstone Park. We were not about to be fazed by a lack of toilets and a little wind and rain. We're Scottish fergoadsakes!

After four hours we'd covered only 26 miles. Lance Armstrong need not quake in his cycle shoes today. But there was no hurry.

We'd no appointments to keep and were carrying food, lights and a tent. No worries.

And then it started. Straight out of a Boris Karloff movie, a perfect multi-pronged lightning bolt punctured the ground a few hundred metres ahead, followed instantly by the loudest BOOM I've ever heard. No counting the seconds between, this was immediate, magnificent and downright terrifying. I thought my time had come. It was the end of the world. Armageddon! Simultaneously, the heavens opened and gigantic raindrops that could take down a buffalo thudded into the earth turning the road into a river. This was rain from the Bible.

Have you ever been so wet that you don't care any more? Saturated, you accept that you can't get any wetter and plunge headlong and carefree into the torrent. You even begin to enjoy it, for a while. As the chill seeps into your bones, you begin to recall that guy in the Public Information film about hypothermia. Remember him? Brain addled by the cold, plodding aimlessly towards a chilling end.

So it was for us. Teeth chattering and in mortal fear of being struck by lightning we struggled onwards, not knowing where or when (or if) we would get respite. The air rumbled and thumped and cracked and fizzled and we sloshed on through the gloom getting colder. And scared.

Then the oddest thing happened. For a moment, I thought it was my life flashing before my eyes. What else could explain it? Dead ahead, through the gloom, I saw us standing at the roadside. Was I looking down at my last moments having left my earthly body? Was this some kind of hypothermia-induced hallucination?

The explanation was much simpler. It was two cyclists dressed exactly like us – right down to the weary look of terrible resignation. Their bikes lay forlornly by the roadside, one of them in pieces.

They couldn't quite believe it either. Our unexpected arrival had clearly terminated an argument and for the first few seconds they seemed suspicious of us. What were these doppelgängers with the strange accents doing out here on this God-forsaken day?

The usual introductory small talk curtailed, we set about repairing their busted bicycle. My father maintains that a tool box needs only two items: 'If it moves and it's not supposed to, use duct tape. If it doesn't move and it's supposed to, WD-40'.

And so, strategically bound tape applied, we splashed on, a bedraggled foursome with kindred spirits renewed. We were soon laughing maniacally at our preposterous plight and, like Lieutenant Dan atop his shrimping boat in *Forrest Gump*, we railed hysterically against the gods, daring them to do their worst.

As this new found euphoria faded, praise be to Thor, Odin and the Canadian National Parks Authority, a wilderness campsite appeared. Without exchanging a word, we made for the toilet block. It was wet, dirty and stank of you-know-what but had a roof and four solid walls. It offered refuge from lightning, wind, rain and bears and it was unanimously agreed; this would do for the night.

Sleeping in a toilet afraid of being eaten by a grizzly. What a great holiday!

But all was not lost. Going outside for the toilet (oh, the irony!) I spotted another building. In our eagerness to get under cover we had missed it. Only a communal kitchen but with tables, chairs and – joy of joys – a huge gas stove, it could have been a presidential suite!

So with gas burners fired up and modesty in front of strangers forgotten, clothes were strung out and emergency rations guzzled.

Outside the storm raged on but we feasted, swapped tales, laughed victoriously and slept on the floor without a care. Brokebike mountain had not broken us.

NO, LUV, WE'RE NOT IN NEW YORK
Kevin Murphy

AS I WAS SAT in the departure lounge two couples sitting next to me with two screaming little girls in tow, I thought, 'God, I hope they don't sit near me on the plane'. The flight was called, as I showed my ticket and passport the stench of body odour nearly knocked me to the floor. I looked round to see where this odour was originating from to find two sweet-looking old ladies smiling at me, I thought, 'God I hope they don't sit next to me on the plane.'

You've probably guessed already, I'm sitting on the plane, I've got two little girls sitting right behind me screaming at the back of my head and the ladies with the personal hygiene problem are sitting right next to me. Why do I get the feeling I'm not going to enjoy this flight? One of the old dears keeps touching me, please make her stop.

We're 20 minutes into the flight and the pilot informs us 'Ladies and gentlemen, I'm afraid we are going to have to turn back to Heathrow, the cargo door light has come on suggesting the cargo door is open.'

'Is that my rucksack I've just seen going past the window?'

So now we're over the Irish Sea emptying the fuel tanks so that we can turn around and land back at Heathrow. The pilot obviously doesn't know what he is doing to my sanity.

There is now no air conditioning and we haven't even been offered a drink, I'm sweating and I'm beginning to wonder if it's me that smells now or is it still the dear old ladies sitting next to me. The pilot has just announced it's going to take another 15 minutes to dump the fuel, 30 minutes to get back to Heathrow and then we're going to have to circle the airport until a space comes up so we can land, then another hour to sort the cargo door and re-fuel again. Now I'm in need of a cigarette.

'God, get me off this plane.'

Holy shit you won't believe this but we have just hit an air pocket and dropped I don't know how far. I've never experienced anything like that before. Everybody let out a big gasp as we fell, I'm sure I saw a couple of people hit their heads on the overhead compartments. I don't believe this, now there has been a massive explosion, this is becoming unbelievable, you couldn't make this up. The pilot has just informed us we have been hit by lightning and that we have nothing to worry about. No word of a lie, for the first time in my life I think that I'm going to die.

We eventually land back at Heathrow and the two old dears sitting next to me think we've arrived in New York! Turns out they can't speak or understand English very well. They never understood any of the tannoys, I tried explaining to them what had happened but I was having my own problems.

It's been nearly two hours since we landed and we don't look any closer to taking off, there is no air conditioning and everybody is now starting to get agitated and smelly.

More bad news, around six people have insisted they be let off the plane, that means more delays as they have to go through all the baggage and pull out the ones that aren't going anywhere. The captain says another half hour. It's getting really hot in here; people are starting to get really agitated. I'm not making this up but Rita Fairclough's stepdaughter has just walked right past me and said hello. Am I hallucinating?

Sweet, one of the little girls has just vomited all over her parents.

Looks as if the flight is going to be cancelled, I'll have to see about sticking a claim in for this. We have sat on the tarmac for God knows how long and gotten absolutely nowhere, things are really getting out of order with some of the passengers, one American couple in particular have risen to the point of hysteria, the female has gone completely cuckoo. I tell her as I head for the toilet she's wasting her time slagging off the stewardesses, as this will achieve nothing. I was wrong about that, by the time I come back out of the toilet they have been bundled off the plane by the police.

That's it then, the flight has been re-scheduled for tomorrow.

After a disturbing night in a flea pit in Earls Court (Wimbledon is on, there isn't a decent hotel room empty for miles) I arrive back at Heathrow to more pandemonium and delays. It turns out it is the same plane as yesterday and people are refusing to get on it.

Advantage me, as a result the plane is more than half empty and I end up enjoying one of the best cross-Atlantic flights I've ever had.

Two weeks into my trip and my mum calls me to tell me there's a letter from British Airways offering me a return ticket anywhere in the world I want. I tell her to get back in touch with them, make it first class and they've got a deal.

COOL DREAMING

Jennifer Syme

SURFING – THE EPITOME of cool, with its image of tanned, blond beings, their grins gleaming as they zoom effortlessly under, through and over the vibrant blue waves, towards golden beaches. The 'dudes', the 'California Girls', the surf boards on top of brightly coloured camper vans, the 'follow the waves' lifestyle. Yes, it is so damn cool.

So here I am, on a cold, rather overcast day clutching a leaflet about 'Learn to Surf' which does have a 'dude' cutting through a massive, impossibly blue wave on the front but looking at the grey-blue sea in the distance, I have to wonder whether it was actually taken on this beach. I wander into the hut/office where a long-haired man grins at me in welcome. Well, at least he looks the part, tanned and muscular, with sun bleached hair tied back in a scraggy pony tail. Then when he speaks, he completes the picture by being Australian, a pure blooded surfer if ever I saw one, probably been on a surf board from the minute he could crawl his way down the beach.

Yes, they have beginners lessons today, surf looks good for it, so he suggests I 'rock along' to the training centre where I'll get kitted out. Having never 'rocked along' in my life, I try to saunter casually in to the other hut where a handful of other pale limbed newbies are struggling into some wet suits. Here I am eyed up by another Australian, but it's all quite innocent as he is merely sizing me for a suit. He then hands me a 'small' which looks like it would be tight on a supermodel, allowing me to feel a mixture of female ego boost joy that he thinks I will fit it, and horrified anticipation as to how I am going to get it on.

I look around for changing rooms but seems like we surfers have no modesty so males and females are all in it together. Oh well, everyone seems too busy with their own suits to worry about catching a glimpse of my wobbly flesh. Once in my swimming costume I nervously examine the suit. It has a zip and a lot of Velcro to undo, with flappy bits inside. I have a quick glance around and note that one person has put the suit on with the zip at the front, which is causing much hilarity amongst the others, so, zip at the back then.

After a fair amount of pushing, squeezing and praying I actually get the suit on and can still breathe, and we set off towards the beach. The five of us who are here for the lesson distinguished from everyone else on the beach by having a) matching wet suits with 'Surf School' emblazoned on the back and b) enormous blue and yellow surf boards. These boards are apparently the surf equivalent of L plates; no real surfer would use them as they are extremely unwieldy and impossible to carry on your own. So just to emphasise that we don't have a clue we have to walk down the beach in twos with one person at the front of the boards and the other bringing up the rear while everyone else skips past carrying small, brightly patterned boards as they run towards the sea.

Ozzie Number One introduces himself as Mike, then gets us to lie on our boards and practise 'popping up' to a stand position. He seems to forget that we are on dry land and everyone can see us as he gets us to 'paddle' our boards and then scramble ourselves in to the surf position, and wave our arms about. I can barely balance on the beach, which doesn't bode well, though I am pleased that I manage not to actually fall off as one girl does.

Now, it's time for the real thing and he leads us down to the sea. There is no time for nerves as a wave rolls in over my legs and splashes my stomach, the water at first icy as it surges through my wet suit, but then once my suit is filled I feel miraculously warm, ready for my first wave.

Ah, the elusive 'perfect wave', now I begin to see why surfing seems to consist mainly of bobbing about, staring out to sea. The waves come so fast, some are too big, some too small; some have little baby ones just in front that if you make the error of trying to ride will sneakily gather themselves into one giant wave and hurl you off the board. Then when a good one does come, everyone wants it and etiquette says one rider per wave so if you are too slow, it's back to bobbing about.

Finally, everyone else has had a go and it's my turn, I struggle on to the board, get myself in position and start paddling as the wave comes up behind me, and I have a brief, exhilarating moment as I am whisked into shore scarily fast, coupled with a strange sensation of being very high up, the other surfers' heads seeming very small and far below. Before I have time to think about this I am abruptly dumped into the shallow water, but my only thought is 'again'.

Second wave, and this time I manage to struggle onto my knees and then, a miracle, as if in slow motion I 'pop up' and I am standing, I am...I stood, I surfed! Mike and the class all whoop and cheer, as I sit in the shallows, my huge board bobbing gently beside me, my head filled with visions of camper vans and beaches and a world waiting to be surfed.

KIDNAP IN THE ALTIPLANO

Ruth Tauber

'wow…'

The first word, so empty of the magnitude of the experience, my shaken hand could pencil so gingerly onto the page of my travel journal in the aftermath of that day.

We had been travelling with friends in Peru for two weeks before then, taking in the magnificent Machu Picchu, and visiting a friend who had been living in this strange country with its thin air and rough, beautiful mountains.

On leaving this friend, we ventured west, to discover in reality the magic that had been promised to us in travellers' tales of Bolivia. The temptation of salt deserts and carnivals concealed any notion of danger.

Before we had even set foot in the country, we were laced up in a scam which was to set our seven week trip to the continent seriously off-course. It began with the chaotic port of Desaguadero, on Peru's border with Bolivia, with the appearance of a young woman in baggy clothes and baseball cap offering to escort us to La Paz.

The minibus journey was uneventful, we picked up other passengers, stopped for fuel and repaired a problem with the bus.

We were soon in La Paz on an unpaved side road. I had thought that perhaps they were to drop off one of the passengers; after all, they did seem on friendly terms. There was a taxi turning into a street to the left. The bus stopped abruptly, men jumped from the taxi brandishing a silver pistol and boarded the bus. In my naivety, I first thought they were after the other passengers, it was some kind of gang affair, and actually felt relieved when one jumped over the seat in front of me, grabbed my hands and pushed me out of sight. I though he was protecting me.

After about 10 minutes the van was parked in a driveway, we were sat up and parcel tape was wrapped roughly round our mouths and hands.

We three were led to a concrete room, glimpsed only through gaps in makeshift blindfolds, pushed down onto hard mattresses and covered with blankets. I could hear the panicked breathing of my companions either side, shallow and stifled. I concentrated on understanding the quickened speech of the men in the room, a welcome distraction from thinking the unthinkable. I could hear our belongings being scattered across the room, valuables and commodities being salvaged. It was not long before they searched us, so thorough that even our socks were removed, checked, and replaced. They found what they wanted, our bank cards, and sat us up one by one, pushing the gun into our mouths and stomachs, to get from us our PIN numbers. Our co-operation saved us from abuse worse than slaps and rough treatment, a fact later confirmed by the tourist police.

When they had gathered the necessary information, some of the party departed to use the bank machine. After what I guessed to be a couple of hours – my own sense of timing was all I could rely on – we could hear our sleeping bags being rolled out. My mind was racing; they were going to move us, but what for? To be shot? To be raped?

Thankfully it was just to be made comfortable for the night. We were frequently offered water, use of a bathroom and food, but I agreed only to the first for fear that any more might be more dangerous.

The time passed in a haze of thoughts of home and family, of the fact that the alert might not be raised for four days, until we were due to meet our friend in Chile, and morbid rationale. Planes passed overhead, our only clue to our geography. Previous to moving us to the other mattress, the twine had been removed from our wrists and parcel tape wrapped around our fingers to make our hands into a prayer position. Surely if they bothered to shake out our fingers and confirm healthy circulation they wouldn't kill us? Yet what possible way out was there?

It soon became clear that things were changing, we were to be moved. I was engaged in a blind conversation with one of our captors, quizzing me about children, husbands and home life, then about where we were to stay in La Paz, and Chile, he was keen that we leave Bolivia as soon as possible.

We were raised up and, still blindfolded, pushed back into the van. By now night had fallen; it was so cold. Still the questions persisted, to a deafening level, where were we going? Sleeping bags were strewn over us. Each of us was being minded by a member of the group, myself by the ringleader. He fumbled in the pocket of his trousers, and my imagination could only race more. Thankfully it was but a grubby Boliviano note, enough for a taxi.

We were pushed out of the mini-van, down to the ground in a heap and again covered in our sleeping bags, two backpacks discarded with us as the little van sped off into the night. After waiting for long enough that we hoped they would be gone, we surfaced.

We walked for some time through the dark, dusty dirt tracks of an industrial estate, with only dogs, the moonlight and the occasional speeding vehicle around. The fear of something even more awful happening to us at that point was, thankfully, cut short by a taxi driver who saw us when occupied but returned to collect us. One by one in the back of the taxi, we broke down, sobbing uncontrollably.

Like so often after a traumatic event, my first thoughts were for my material possessions, my journals, photos of home, and beautiful words written in cards by friends who felt so far away then. But when we had finally reached the safety of a hotel we opened the packs returned to us to find our passports, bankcards, some clothes, documents and that travel journal...

THE TALKEETNA GOOD TIMES

Emma Turnbull

SOMETIMES ONE DAY is enough time to get a flavour of somewhere, sometimes it isn't enough to even get past the first page of a place. I had a day in a little town called Talkeetna, and it was long enough to know I would always yearn to be there, a little.

I arrived in Alaska in a heat wave, on my first day I met a man walking two enormous dogs, he called out to me, 'I can see you checking out my shorts, well – you're right, these ain't shorts, these is underwear, I don't own no shorts, it's never BEEN this hot in Anchorage.' I knew then that Alaska was going to be great.

Two days later three of us decided to go to Mount McKinley, Talkeetna was the nearest town. There was a rumour that the TV series *Northern Exposure* was based on Talkeetna, that it had umpteen quirky locals and plenty of oddball happenings. It sounded ace.

We arrived mid-morning and found there were only two spaces left on the tourist flight around Mount McKinley. Being the least passionate about tiny planes I opted out and wandered off to discover small town Alaska on my own.

It was too hot for any major exploring so I wound my way down to the river and sat to read a book in the shade. I sat breathing the clean air and basking in the complete and perfect solitude. I had noticed a collection of tents and camper vans on the river banks. As I sat there dipping my toes in the water a gathering noise began to emerge from the makeshift settlement and then, suddenly, a horde of naked hippies came hurtling out and went whooping down into the water. They shrieked and swam and splashed about all big and liberated. It was one of those moments when you feel like the life you should have had is being shown to you on a cinema screen in heaven and God is saying, 'Why didn't you join in, pet?' I tried not to look at all the nakedness and attempted to cultivate an 'I too am liberated and cool but today I am expressing it by reading quietly – no I'm not a Nanna-before-my-time' type of look, it was quite hard to pull off. Anyway it didn't matter because the naked hippies weren't looking, they were too busy living.

After a while I sloped off to meet my pals to drive back to

Anchorage. They were quite flustered and explained that the car keys had vanished. There followed a whole afternoon walking like someone who had been punched in the guts. Walking like that attracts attention and before long ten passers-by were slumped over scouring the key-less ground of the town. We (literally) bumped into someone from Talkeetna radio and they broadcast the news about the missing keys. By mid-afternoon it seemed like half the town was doubled over. As we searched we saw little hand-painted houses with vegetables in the garden, lumberjacks, a pretty school with singing kids, a disused train line, people chatting and laughing on the way back from the grocers. It was kind of idyllic and the locals kept finding things that were better than keys but then it started to get dark and cold and a bit of panic started to seep in at the edges.

We went back to the flight centre and a crinkle-faced old cowboy was there, he had retired from his money-making life to fly tourists around a big mountain in Northern Alaska. Talking to him I suddenly knew that everything would be OK. He told us stories about his two lives (before and after the move to Alaska) and told us we could sleep in the bunk house where the pilots stayed.

The bunkhouse was very basic and uncomfortable but it didn't matter, it was warm and safe and despite being there on our own there was a tangible sense of community. We went out for food and found sweet little buns in a little late night bakery. We sat chatting to key-searchers from the day and looking into the dark. It was nothing amazing, nothing life changing but it was one of those little feelings of home you sometimes long for when you're not there.

I lay in my bunk that night and fantasised about a Talkeetna life, I imagined dropping out and doing something wholesome and good. Before I went to sleep I read the local newspaper, the *Talkeetna Good Times*. It carried stories from the town and news pieces about Alaska. On the back page was a short story by a local writer. Entitled *Cold*, it was about winter in Talkeetna. It spoke about sitting in a room watching a door knob grow thicker and thicker with frost and hearing trees crack as the water inside them froze solid, throwing coffee out of the door and seeing it freeze in mid-air. It talked about moving closer and closer to the fire as the night moved on and seemed to move in. I was completely mesmerised and suddenly understood something about cramming the summer full of life, I wondered if maybe the people were so warm here because they really understood the dangers of being too cold.

The next morning the break down company broke us into the car. Before they arrived I went to the offices of the newspaper and bought a *Talkeetna Good Times* T-shirt.

Every time I wear it I remember the support of strangers and that sense of community spirit, mixed with the promise of cold.

Index of Authors

Luath Press Limited
committed to publishing well written books worth reading

LUATH PRESS takes its name from Robert Burns, whose little collie Luath (*Gael.*, swift or nimble) tripped up Jean Armour at a wedding and gave him the chance to speak to the woman who was to be his wife and the abiding love of his life. Burns called one of 'The Twa Dogs' Luath after Cuchullin's hunting dog in Ossian's *Fingal*. Luath Press was established in 1981 in the heart of Burns country, and is now based a few steps up the road from Burns' first lodgings on Edinburgh's Royal Mile.

Luath offers you distinctive writing with a hint of unexpected pleasures.

Most bookshops in the UK, the US, Canada, Australia, New Zealand and parts of Europe either carry our books in stock or can order them for you. To order direct from us, please send a £sterling cheque, postal order, international money order or your credit card details (number, address of cardholder and expiry date) to us at the address below. Please add post and packing as follows: UK – £1.00 per delivery address; overseas surface mail – £2.50 per delivery address; overseas airmail – £3.50 for the first book to each delivery address, plus £1.00 for each additional book by airmail to the same address. If your order is a gift, we will happily enclose your card or message at no extra charge.

Luath Press Limited
543/2 Castlehill
The Royal Mile
Edinburgh EH1 2ND
Scotland
Telephone: 0131 225 4326 (24 hours)
Fax: 0131 225 4324
email: sales@luath.co.uk
Website: www.luath.co.uk